A Practical Guide to Teaching Foreign Languages in the Secondary School

How can you effectively motivate young people to engage with foreign language learning?

How can young people engage with new ideas and cultural experiences within and outside the classroom?

The new edition of *A Practical Guide to Teaching Foreign Languages in the Secondary School* offers straightforward advice and inspiration for training teachers, NQTs and teachers in their early professional development. Written by a team of expert professionals, it offers a wide range of strategies for successful teaching in the languages classroom. Key topics covered include:

- helping pupils develop better listening skills;
- effective speaking activities;
- choosing the best texts and technology for reading skills;
- teaching grammar;
- internet tools and services for teaching and learning;
- integrating formative assessment;
- the intercultural dimension of language teaching;
- collaborating with primary schools and successful transition;
- teaching Arabic and Mandarin;
- working with TAs and FLAs;
- classroom research and reflective practice.

This fully revised and updated second edition includes new chapters on homework, motivation and less widely taught languages, while the core sections on reading and writing, planning, and culture and diversity have been significantly updated to reflect important changes in research, practice and policy.

A Practical Guide to Teaching Foreign Languages in the Secondary School extends the popular *Learning to Teach Foreign Languages in the Secondary School* by providing detailed examples of theory in practice, based on the most up-to-date research and practice, as well as links to relevant sources supporting evidence-informed practice. It is an essential compendium of support and ideas for all those embarking upon their first steps in a successful career in teaching foreign languages.

Norbert Pachler is Professor of Education at the Institute of Education, University of London, UK.

Ana Redondo is Senior Lecturer in Education and Subject Leader, Secondary PGCE in Modern Languages at the University of Bedfordshire, UK.

Routledge Teaching Guides
Series Editors: Susan Capel and Marilyn Leask

These Practical Guides have been designed as companions to **Learning to Teach X Subject in the Secondary School**. For information on the Routledge Teaching Guides series please visit our website at www.routledge.com/education.

New titles to support you throughout your early career as a foreign languages teacher

Learning to Teach Foreign Languages in the Secondary School, 4th edition
Norbert Pachler, Michael Evans, Ana Redondo and Linda Fisher

This essential textbook is established as the leading title for those learning to teach foreign languages in the secondary school. Now fully revised in its fourth edition, it applies the underpinning theory to practical issues and covers key concepts and skills.

PB ISBN: 978-0-415-68996-0 (2013)

Debates in Modern Languages Education
Edited by Patricia Driscoll, Ernesto Macaro and Ann Swarbrick

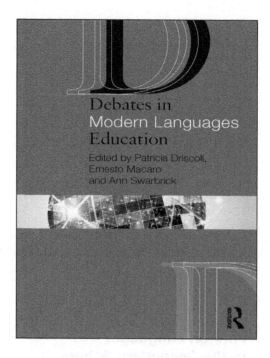

The *Debates* series offers in one place an accessible, authoritative introduction to the key themes, issues and tensions in your field. It supports you in reaching your own informed judgements, enabling you to discuss and argue your point of view with deeper theoretical knowledge and understanding. Essential reading for those engaged in initial teacher education, continuing professional development and Masters level study.

PB ISBN: 978-0-415-65833-1 (2013)

A Practical Guide to Teaching Foreign Languages in the Secondary School

Second Edition

**Edited by Norbert Pachler
and Ana Redondo**

Routledge
Taylor & Francis Group

LONDON AND NEW YORK

Second edition published 2014
by Routledge
2 Park Square, Milton Park, Abingdon, Oxon OX14 4RN

and by Routledge
711 Third Avenue, New York, NY 10017

Routledge is an imprint of the Taylor & Francis Group, an informa business

First edition published by Routledge 2007

British Library Cataloguing in Publication Data
A catalogue record for this book is available from the British Library

Library of Congress Cataloging in Publication Data
A practical guide to teaching foreign languages in the secondary school / edited
by Norbert Pachler and Ana Redondo. -- Second Edition.
pages cm. -- (Routledge teaching guides)
1. Languages, Modern--Study and teaching (Secondary) I. Pachler, Norbert. II.
Redondo, Ana. III. Title: Teaching modern foreign languages in the secondary
school.
PB35.T424 2014
418.0071'2--dc23
2013037757

ISBN: 978-0-415-63332-1 (pbk)
ISBN: 978-0-203-09511-9 (ebk)

Typeset in Palatino and Frutiger
by Saxon Graphics Ltd, Derby

Contents

Contributors

Jim Anderson is Senior Lecturer in Languages in Education at Goldsmiths, University of London. He coordinates the innovative PGCE course in Arabic, Bengali, Mandarin, Panjabi and Urdu and leads a Masters module on 'Language in Multilingual Contexts'. His research focuses on the development of inclusive and integrated approaches to language learning in schools.

Amanda Barton is Honorary Lecturer in Education at the School of Education, University of Manchester, working on the PGCE in MFL. She is a member of the Editorial Advisory Board for *The Language Learning Journal* and her publications address gender differences in language learning, the teaching of languages in primary school and the retention of new teachers.

Nalini Boodhoo is Head of the School of Education at the University of East Anglia where she is also the Academic Director for the primary and secondary Modern Foreign Languages PGCE courses. She sits on the Editorial Board of the Cambridge Journal of Education.

Elspeth Broady was formerly Head of Languages, Literature and Communication at the University of Brighton. Her interests lie in language teaching materials design, the teaching of grammar and second language acquisition. She now works as a freelance educational consultant and is joint editor of *The Language Learning Journal*.

Mike Calvert is Head of Department, Children, Young People and Education in the Faculty of Education and Theology at York St John University.

Gary Chambers is Associate Professor at the School of Education, University of Leeds. He is Head of the Secondary PGCE course and a former editor of *The Language Learning Journal*.

Sue Field has worked as Senior Lecturer in Education (MFL) at Canterbury Christ Church University, as Associate Editor of the Teacher Training Resource Bank, and as an Academic Associate with the Higher Education Academy. She is currently completing a Doctorate in Education.

Suzanne Graham is Professor of Language and Education at the Institute of Education, University of Reading. She is Subject Leader for the MFL Initial Teacher Education course and the Institute Director of Research.

Prue Holmes is Senior Lecturer in the School of Education, Durham University. She teaches and leads a programme in intercultural education. Her research includes a European multilateral project to develop an intercultural pathway for Erasmus students studying abroad (IEREST) (http://ierest-project.eu/) and researching multilingually (http://researchingmultilingually.com/).

Marilyn Hunt was Associate Professor of Teacher Education at the University of Warwick until 2010. Her current post is Curriculum Tutor at Oxford University Department of Education. Her research interests include primary languages, assessment and CLIL.

Elisabeth Lazarus is a Senior Lecturer in Education (MFL) at the Graduate School of Education, University of Bristol. For many years she was Subject Coordinator for MFL and is currently Co-Director of all Masters programmes which the GSoE offers in Bristol and Hong Kong.

Lynne Meiring is Senior Lecturer in Education at Swansea Metropolitan University School of Education with particular responsibility for modern foreign languages. Prior to that she taught languages to adults and in industry, and has experience as a language consultant as well as an ESTYN section 10 and independent school inspector.

Trevor Mutton is currently PGCE Course Director and an MFL subject tutor at the University of Oxford. His research interests focus primarily on the professional learning of beginning teachers.

Nigel Norman was formerly Senior Lecturer in Education at Swansea Metropolitan University School of Education. His research interests include grammar in language teaching, and information technology in languages. He was reviews editor for *The Language Learning Journal*.

Norbert Pachler is Professor of Education at the Institute of Education, University of London. He is the convenor of the London Mobile Learning Group (http://www.londonmobilelearning.net) and joint editor of *The Language Learning Journal* published by Routledge.

Ana Redondo is Senior Lecturer in Education and Subject Leader of a Secondary PGCE in Modern Languages. She is co-author of the fourth edition of 'Learning to teach foreign languages in the Secondary school' (London: Routledge, 2013).

Thomas Strasser is New Learning Technologies Researcher, teacher trainer at Vienna University College of Teacher Education, ELT textbook author and international speaker. He is a member of scientific committees for various journals and conferences in the field of TEL, Social Media, ePortfolios. For details, see http://www.learning-reloaded.com

Series editors' introduction

This practical work book is part of a series of textbooks for student teachers called the *Routledge Teaching Guides*. It complements and extends the popular generic book entitled *Learning to Teach in the Secondary School: A Companion to School Experience*, as well as the subject specific book *Learning to Teach Foreign Languages in the Secondary School*. We anticipate that you will want to use this book in conjunction with these other books.

Teaching is rapidly becoming a more research and evidence informed profession. Research and professional evidence about good practice underpins the *Learning to Teach in the Secondary School* series and these practical work books. Both the generic and subject specific books in the *Learning to Teach in the Secondary School* series provide theoretical, research and professional evidence-based advice and guidance to support you as you focus on developing aspects of your teaching or your pupils' learning as you progress through your initial teacher education course and beyond. Although the generic and subject specific books include some case studies and tasks to help you consider the issues, the practical application of material is not their major focus. That is the role of this book.

This book aims to reinforce your understanding of aspects of your teaching, support you in aspects of your development as a teacher and your teaching, and enable you to analyse your success as a teacher in maximising pupils' learning by focusing on practical applications. The practical activities in this book can be used in a number of ways. Some activities are designed to be undertaken by you individually, others as a joint task in pairs and yet others as group work working with, for example, other student teachers or a school or university-based tutor. Your tutor may use the activities with a group of student teachers. The book has been designed so that you can write directly into it.

In England, you have a range of colleagues to support in your classroom. They also provide an additional resource on which you can draw. In any case, you will, of course, need to draw on additional resources to support your development. Other resources are available on a range of websites, including that for *Learning to Teach in the Secondary School: A Companion to School Experience: 6th Edition* (www.routledge.com/cw/Capel), which lists key websites for Scotland, Wales, Northern Ireland and England.

We do hope that this practical work book is useful in supporting your development as a teacher. We welcome feedback which can be incorporated into future editions.

Susan Capel
Marilyn Leask
Series Editors

Chapter 1   Foreign language teaching

Understanding approaches, making choices[1]

ELSPETH BROADY

BY THE END OF THIS CHAPTER YOU SHOULD:

- understand some of the key challenges involved in foreign language (FL) learning and teaching;
- have reflected on the key aims for FL teaching in secondary schools;
- be aware of how approaches to language teaching may differ, and of their advantages and disadvantages;
- have explored the rationale for target language (TL) and first language (L1) use in the classroom;
- have considered via some practical activities how these debates apply to FL teaching and learning.

THERE IS NO IDEAL WAY TO TEACH A LANGUAGE

Whenever you read or hear about the teaching and learning of FLs, you learn that there is no definitive answer to the question of how people learn a FL. Some swear that you can only learn by immersion in the TL; others emphasise the importance of understanding how the TL grammar works. Some can pick up TL words from just listening; others need to see words written down. You, of course, will have your own view and preferences, based on your personal experience of language learning. But as a teacher, you are going to be working with a range of individuals, all of whom will bring different experiences, learning styles, preferences and motivations to language learning. Furthermore, despite a large body of knowledge on the various factors involved in language learning, there is no ready-made, 'one-size-fits-all' teaching recipe to follow with guaranteed results for all.

This apparent lack of clarity may feel daunting at first; it means that as teachers, *we* have to make the choices about how best to promote language learning given the needs and interests of our pupils. We have to do this in an informed and principled way, interpreting carefully the advice and research available, as well as the various legislative requirements, official guidelines and recommended frameworks that surround everyday teaching. But teaching FLs nevertheless offers scope for considerable creativity. This chapter – and indeed all the chapters in this book – aim(s) to help you understand key principles underpinning FL teaching, so that you can build your professional practice on a well-informed and thoughtful foundation.

Task 1.1

Reflecting on FL learning and teaching experiences

This task is best undertaken first as individual reflection, followed by discussion with others. Do you see things the same or differently from other people in your teacher development group?

- Think back over your own classroom learning of a FL. What kinds of classroom activities helped you? Were there any that hindered you? Why?
- Do you remember a particularly inspirational FL teacher? What was it that they did that made a difference to you as a learner?
- Note down some of the kinds of classroom activities you would particularly like to try out as a classroom FL teacher. What do you think are the possible advantages and disadvantages of these activities? Will they work with all pupils?

Typically, different approaches to language teaching have tended to emphasise *either* building knowledge of the *forms* of language in the hope that the ability to communicate *meaning* will then develop of its own accord, or conversely, emphasising the communication of *meaning*, on the assumption that learners will pick up the forms of the language inductively. Both approaches have known successes and failures. However, as this chapter aims to make clear, this polarisation is neither necessary nor desirable in the context of school-based FL teaching.

It has sometimes been argued that FL learning should be most effective if it can mimic a 'natural' approach, involving immersion in the TL and avoiding all reference to a learner's other languages. After all, this is how we learn our L1, and many of us have experience of 'picking up' a second language (L2) through residence abroad. But think how different those contexts are from a school classroom. No matter how hard we try, we cannot re-create that level of on-going interaction with the TL in three 45-minute periods a week. With no prior knowledge to help, picking up a language inductively in this way takes a long time and, indeed, it can be stressful.

Furthermore, secondary level pupils come to FL learning with extensive knowledge and skills in their first (and sometimes other) language(s), as well as a range of cognitive learning skills. It surely does not make sense to teach a FL without any reference to these. Yet to teach a FL just as some kind of abstract language system to be learned through the medium of the L1 also makes little sense. Reciting verb paradigms and learning lists of decontextualized vocabulary through translation can feel horribly divorced from any reality; its meaninglessness is demotivating for most pupils. Our job as teachers is to find the right balance of form and meaning, learning and using, and L1 and TL use.

The challenge, however you look at it, is that learning a FL takes time and motivation. There are potentially an infinite number of words and structures to be learned, and, like any skill, being able to use a FL takes practice. We have to build up our communicative 'performance' gradually; our initial efforts may be awkward and embarrassing, particularly as we are used to communicating effectively in our L1, and much of the practice may feel repetitive. In the school setting, pupils do not have an infinite amount of time; nor can we assume their motivation. As FL teachers, therefore, we need to think carefully about how best to use the opportunities we have to build on our learners' abilities. We need to be clear what we want learners to achieve and to set both realistic and ambitious goals for our pupils.

UNDERSTANDING THE AIMS OF FL TEACHING

So what should be the aims of FL learning in secondary schools? Most of us would probably say first that we want learners to be able to use the TL. We want them to be able to understand, and be understood, in both speech and writing; we want them to be able to communicate successfully with other users of the TL. That, after all, is what language is for. Furthermore, we probably want to specify that learners should be able to communicate their own personal meanings and develop curiosity and insight into aspects of the lives and culture(s) of TL speakers. Without this, there can be little motivation for language learning. It has been recognised that learning a FL can help pupils become more aware of how different cultural groups think, live and express themselves, and thus come to understand and value cultural diversity – an important social aim.

But if learners are to be able to create their own phrases in the TL, and get to grips with 'real' language from the TL culture(s), then we also need to equip our learners with an understanding of how the TL works. As we explore below, insight into language structure is increasingly seen as significant in facilitating classroom language learning. Without it, language learning risks being reduced to mere parroting of set phrases.

Furthermore, learners need to have some idea about how to go about FL learning so that they can become more independent learners and, consequently, more independent users of the TL. As we mentioned earlier, there is a lot to learn in learning a FL, and it cannot all be 'taught' directly; secondly, different learners are likely to have different preferences, different strengths and different orientations. Helping learners understand their options for learning is an important way of engaging them as individuals and building their motivation.

Task 1.2

Aims of FL learning

Look at some of the current statutory specifications for FLs, such as the *2014 National Curriculum Programme of Study for FLs* at https://www.education.gov. uk/schools/teachingandlearning/curriculum/nationalcurriculum2014, and identify to what extent – and how – the aims presented above are expressed. Would you like to add any other aims?

HOW DO WE BUILD UP ABILITY TO USE THE TL?

So if we want learners to be able to *use* the TL, let us just think for a moment what developing even minimal communicative ability in an L2 actually requires. Before learners can produce anything, they need 'input'. We often forget that comprehension is primary in L2 learning; only through exposure to the TL can learners begin to familiarise themselves with the patterns of its sounds, words and grammatical structure. But what should this 'input' be? If we 'throw learners in at the deep end' and try to engage them immediately with extensive TL use, some may rise to the challenge but many will feel they are drowning. Just trying to process TL sounds, let alone understanding words, can be far more challenging for beginning learners than we, as expert users of that language, realise.

Task 1.3

Making sense of an unfamiliar language

You are visiting the Netherlands and know virtually no Dutch. You decide to buy some things in a department store. All goes well at the cash desk until the cashier says to you something which sounds like / *spartuairmulsmuvrow* / in a rising intonation which you interpret as a question.

- Can you guess from the context what she might be saying?
- Can you guess any words within the string of sounds?
- Assuming you really have no idea what she's saying, what would you want to say back in Dutch in this situation?

Key to Task 1.3

1. The phrase is not the obvious question we might predict in a shopping exchange such as *Would you like a plastic bag*? It actually means *Do you collect Air Miles, Madam*? I have used this example to highlight how difficult it can sometimes be to guess from context, even in contexts which appear to be very similar to ones we know well.

2. Now you know the meaning of the phrase, can you segment the string of sounds? You may identify / *airmuls* / as 'Air Miles'. You might also identify / *muvrow* / as 'Madam', particularly if you know some German: / *vrow* / sounds like the German word for woman, *Frau*. It's easier to guess if you see the question written down: *Spaart u Air Miles mevrouw?* You can probably now work out that *u* is the Dutch for 'you', which only leaves *Spaart*. Linked to 'Air Miles', this must mean 'save'. Without seeing the written form, it can be hard to identify where TL words begin and end. Without that segmentation, it's hard to work out both what the individual words mean and how they are assembled together.

In some contexts, of course, it is quite possible to guess accurately at meaning even where we have no or little knowledge of the language involved. When a waiter in a Dutch café says *Dank u wel* after you have paid your bill, it does not take much to guess that he is saying 'Thank you'. When he adds, *Tot ziens* as you walk out the door, you can be pretty sure it is some kind of leave-taking expression equivalent to 'Bye'. And, of course, it is true that there is a lot you can do as a teacher to make the meaning of new TL input clear – gestures, flash-cards, visuals of all kinds can help clarify, as can simple translation. Encouraging guess-work is particularly important to build learners' own strategies for coping with the TL. But then the next step is for learners to move from understanding the general meaning of a TL expression to retaining it with reasonable accuracy. Most learners require a great deal of practice and repetition before they can produce an expression accurately, and then use it appropriately in a new situation. Making that practice interesting and challenging is a key task for FL teachers, particularly in anglophone environments where most learners will only meet the TL in the classroom.

You might think that language teaching could just focus on building up learners' recognition and production of a number of useful set phrases like *Hello, how are you? I'm fine, thanks, and you? Could I have a Coke, please? How much is that?* There would be no need to know what the component elements meant; just when the phrases were used and vaguely what they meant. But think about how limited that TL knowledge would be. Language is designed to be 'creative', to allow speakers to produce utterances that are not mere communicative tokens. Though language use can be predictable, as we saw in the café example, much of it is not, as we saw in Task 1.3 – and in any case, it is hard to predict appropriately exactly where and how our learners might want to use the target language. Criticism of early versions of the GCSE FL syllabuses, for example, highlighted the absurdity of requiring 16 year olds to learn phrases for asking for petrol in a garage, or play the part of a traffic policeman.

So while it is no doubt helpful for learners to learn set communicative phrases – *Hello, Good-bye, Thank-you, Excuse-me, I'm sorry, I don't understand* – they also need the knowledge to move beyond these set phrases; both in order to understand a wider range of TL texts, and to produce their own phrases which are not simply parroted repetitions. For example, learners of French need to see there are common elements in phrases such as *Je **ne** comprends **pas*** and *Je **n'aime pas*** which they may have learned as chunks. These common elements can be used to create 'new' phrases by being applied to other chunks: *Je veux -> **Je ne veux pas**, Je peux ->**Je ne peux pas***. Taking a Spanish example, a key element in the question, *¿Donde vives?* can reoccur in the answer *Vivo en Londres*. Just realising that the first part of the key word stays the same, while the ending changes depending on who the word relates to, is a powerful insight: it is the key to using other verbs.

Formal grammar gives names to these 'common elements' such as personal pronouns (*Je* in French, *u* in Dutch), negative particles (*ne … pas*), verb stems (*viv-*) and verb endings (*-o, -es* etc. in Spanish, *-t* in Dutch). It is arguable that these names can help us understand how the structures of a language work, and thus develop the knowledge required to use a language. This belief was certainly emphasised in the grammar translation approach to language teaching, which was influential from the nineteenth to the late twentieth century. The problem, however, is that, divorced from meaningful language use, the grammatical concepts behind these terms can feel so abstract that they hinder, rather than help. Most of us tend to find it easier, and more motivating, to hear phrases in the TL in some kind of context, to try to work out what they mean, to practise saying them and *then* explore their structure.

Naming structures and analysing them in isolation may help more once forms are familiar in use. Making connections with other language(s) is also useful in confirming and reinforcing our understanding. Helping learners crack the language code can certainly engage their intellectual curiosity and develop their analytic skills, as well as build explicit knowledge that can support their TL use. However, it is worth remembering that explicit language knowledge can be difficult to access quickly in performance: having to check every ending on every verb as you go along is unlikely to promote fluency!

As we develop our familiarity and understanding of how structures function, so we can begin to use them ourselves, and we can start to be more 'creative', using them with a broader range of vocabulary in a wider range of contexts. As we mentioned earlier, 'performing' language fluently in real time takes time to build up, approximation after approximation, through lots and lots of practice. Most secondary learners are used to being savvy and individual communicators in their L1; being reduced to uttering simple (and often banal) phrases awkwardly in the TL can be very demotivating. What can be very motivating is the sense of cracking the code and accessing a different culture, and, of course, successfully getting your message across: communicating.

In summary, learning to use a FL involves making sense of TL input, spotting recurrent patterns of both sound and structure, learning to reproduce and extend these patterns, collecting a stock of words, and using these resources in real time to communicate with others.

Task 1.4

Typical sequences of learning activities

Look at the sequence of learning activities below.

1 Learners hear ten items presented in a logical order with visuals.
2 They may, almost simultaneously, see the written forms.
3 They understand the meanings.
4 They repeat the items sufficient times to feel confident with the pronunciation.
5 They practise these items through a variety of activities, involving more demanding cognitive processes where possible.
6 They use them to communicate a message to others.

- In your chosen TL, expand each stage by adding relevant vocabulary and tasks as appropriate.
- What is the *purpose* of each step? Could you imagine other ways of achieving this purpose?
- Explore the extent to which this sequence reflects the typical sequencing of activities in a FL coursebook you are familiar with.

DIFFERENT APPROACHES TO LANGUAGE TEACHING, DIFFERENT CHOICES

Generations of language teachers and researchers have reflected on how best to support language learning, but as we mentioned at the outset, nobody has come up with the perfect 'method'. Many language teachers throughout the world now claim allegiance to Communicative Language Teaching (CLT), a broad approach based on recognition that learners need to develop the ability to communicate in the TL, and not just a passive knowledge of vocabulary, structure and grammar rules. This emphasis reflects much of our discussion above about what the aims of FL secondary teaching should be.

However, CLT has been associated with a lot of controversy, and indeed misunderstanding. For example, it has been assumed that CLT requires that the TL be used at all times in the classroom; that formal grammar and error correction be banished because they undermine the development of TL skills; and that all learning activities in the classroom should mimic 'real life'. It is true that CLT has been underpinned by research and reflection in the study of second language acquisition (SLA) which has tended to emphasise the role of implicit learning, where TL knowledge builds up primarily through meaningful interaction. More recently, however, the role of explicit learning of language forms – or at the very least, the conscious 'noticing' of forms – has been shown to be significant in helping learners develop their language abilities, and there is also evidence to suggest that judicious use of learners' L1 (or normal language of instruction) can be facilitative of learning, rather than a hindrance.

At first glance, it seems self-evident that the TL should predominate in the FL classroom, given what we have said about the limited exposure pupils in the UK have to FLs. How else will learners feel challenged to take that leap into using the TL? But conversely, being forced to listen to language you do not understand, denied the ability to react or intervene in any way, is intensely demotivating. Furthermore, as we have noted above, most of us will instinctively link and check new words and expressions we have learned back to our L1, or other languages we know. This not only helps us develop our knowledge of the TL, but also builds our knowledge about language in general. And let us not forget that the skill of translating the TL into our L1 is in itself a real communicative skill that can be particularly useful, and bring a sense of value to FL knowledge. We also know that being able to *discuss* our learning with others – explore what we understand, discuss what we do not understand, share anxieties and understand our progress – is itself important, and most pupils will want to do that in their L1. There are thus important activities in FL learning where L1 use is entirely appropriate.

TL use by the teacher is clearly important for maximising learners' TL exposure and creating the expectation that learners themselves should take the plunge to communicate in the TL. TL routines, for example, can and should be established in the classroom, but it is important to help learners feel in control by ensuring that TL phrases equivalent to *I don't understand, Please could you repeat? What does that mean?* are well-known or can be easily accessed from wall posters. The idea is to make the TL feel a normal part of communication in the classroom. Bear in mind, though, that requiring learners to *produce* the TL may block them from developing their ability to *understand* it; asking learners to say in English what they think you – or another speaker – have just said in the TL can engage curiosity and willingness to guess. A useful technique can be to get learners to interpret for each other. Understanding the TL is *using* it, even if that understanding is then expressed in English. If you can get pupils to see using the TL in different ways as a series of surmountable challenges, then it is much more likely to be motivating rather than intimidating.

As for making learning activities 'realistic', we know now how easily this can be misinterpreted: there is nothing motivating per se about having learners 'order meals they are not going to eat, plan journeys they are not going to make and hear about people they are not going to meet' (Grenfell, 2000: 24). 'Realistic' is not necessarily 'relevant' to learners' needs and interests, and it is the sense of relevance that underlies motivation.

It may well be the case that getting learners to use their TL to 'do' something with their language knowledge, such as creating an animation using simple conversational phrases or contributing to a class blog, *is* more stimulating than completing gap-fill exercises. Learning through doing can certainly provide a rewarding sense of an end product; we strive to achieve an outcome, and the outcome tells us we have achieved something. Yet we should not forget that before learners can 'do', they often feel the need to 'learn' and 'practise'. Littlewood (1981) usefully distinguished between 'communicative' activities where pupils 'do' something with language, and 'pre-communicative' activities where they focus on learning and practising the language they will later require for 'doing'.

Task 1.5

Pre-communicative and communicative activities

Read the definition below and decide whether the activities in the list are 'pre-communicative' or communicative? Or could they be both?

'Pre-communicative activities focus on linguistic structures or vocabulary items. Communicative activities require learners to put into use the structures and vocabulary they have been practising for communication.'

(Morgan and Neil, 2001, p. 7)

1 Practising a written dialogue acting out various emotions
2 Chanting
3 Pair work
4 Group work
5 Surveys
6 Role play
7 Interviewing a partner
8 Filling in the gaps worksheet
9 Guessing unknown vocabulary in a reading text
10 True/false activity
11 Making a presentation
12 Language games
13 Listening for gist/detail
14 Expressing opinions
15 Planning/carrying out group activities
16 Producing creative texts
17 Choosing a holiday from a brochure
18 Describing the ideal holiday

A recent variant of CLT, Task-based Language Learning (TBLL), emphasises language learning through 'doing' and encourages teachers to organise their lessons around 'tasks'. A task is an activity which 'seeks to engage learners in using language … require[ing] a primary focus on meaning' (Ellis, 2003: 9). As such, it involves some kind of 'gap' which learners have to close using language. For example, it might be finding out from a partner where they spent their summer holidays, or pooling information from different sources to complete a questionnaire. The idea is that the task can be designed in order to encourage relevant practice, while at the same time giving the learners the feeling that they are 'doing' something. For instance, a simple task for practising classroom vocabulary might involve learners each receiving a drawing of a certain number of classroom items. They then try to find others with exactly the same drawing by asking each other questions, *Do you have a …?* The task could be made more complex by making information about the position of the objects important: *In the first row, is there a book? Is there a ruler on the left?*

Key dimensions for determining tasks are *complexity*, *accuracy* and *fluency*. *Complexity* refers to the range of language – vocabulary and structure – that a learner uses. *Accuracy* refers to the degree to which the language used is correct, and *fluency* refers to the appropriate speed of TL delivery, the absence of pauses and breakdowns which impair communication. These three things are all important in becoming an effective language user, but achieving all three requires a great deal of skill. The idea is that teachers can design tasks to prioritise different aspects at different times, depending on what they expect their learners to achieve. For example, at the initial stages of language learning, you might want to emphasise fluency rather than accuracy in oral work: just getting learners to produce an appropriate TL phrase which is understandable, if not totally correct. Gradually, you can increase expectations. If learners are re-using vocabulary and structures they are familiar with, then you can expect greater accuracy. As their knowledge builds up, so you can challenge them to produce more complex language. For example, in answer to routine questions such as *What do you enjoy doing at the weekend?*, you can insist that learners not only say what they enjoy, but why.

Exponents of TBLL have tended to suggest that language learning is best served when learners are encouraged to try out a task first, mobilising their existing language resources to complete it successfully, and then reflect on how they could improve their performance. This 'deep-end' strategy can be useful where learners have already built up some TL resources. TBLL, however, does acknowledge that language teaching can involve 'exercises' (where learners focus on learning and form-focused practising – Littlewood's 'pre-communicative' activities) as well as meaning-focused tasks.

Whether the approach to language teaching implied in statutory FL specifications is explicitly termed 'communicative' or not, it is likely to espouse the following communicative aims:

a   to get learners to engage with (i.e. receive and produce) meaningful messages;
b   to help learners to develop language skills through practical activities with a purpose;
c   to encourage learners to use a range of communication strategies to make sense of the TL and to get their meaning across;
d   to help learners recognise that language may be used differently in different contexts and for different purposes.

Within this framework, what is key for you as a teacher is to think carefully about the purpose of the learning activities you decide to use; when you plan, you need to think carefully and critically how each activity contributes to building up learners' knowledge and skills in the TL.

Task 1.6

Range of FL activities

Look at the verbs below. They could all conceivably be used in lesson plans to show what the pupils and you will be doing.

Collaborate	Listen	Imagine	Use
Act out	Create	Present	Predict
Revise	Highlight	Describe	Learn
Exemplify	Elicit	Guess	Chant
List	Enunciate	Demonstrate	Choose
Copy	Suggest	Repeat	Read
Prioritise	Read	Memorise	Check
Decide	Deduce	Summarise	Spot

- What pupil learning and thinking is implied with each verb?
- In lessons you have observed or taught, how many of these verbs could have been used to describe what pupils were doing?
- Which other verbs have you seen exemplified in MFL classrooms?
- Are there any you would like to add which you haven't encountered in practice?

As we have seen, different approaches to language teaching may argue for different emphases in teaching. What you have to judge is which of the many teaching options available to you is most appropriate to your learners and your context.

NOTES

1 Based on: Barnes, A. (2007) 'Communicative approaches to modern foreign language teaching and using the target language'. In Pachler, N. and Redondo, A. (eds) (2007) *A Practical Guide to Teaching Modern Foreign Languages in the Secondary School.* London: Routledge, pp. 4–11.

REFERENCES

Ellis, R. (2003) 'Tasks in SLA and language pedagogy', in Ellis, R. (ed.) *Task-based Language Learning and Teaching.* Oxford: Oxford University Press, pp. 1–35.

Grenfell, M. (2000) 'Modern languages: beyond Nuffield and into the 21st century'. *The Language Learning Journal*, 22(1), 23–29.

Littlewood, W. (1981) *Communicative Language Teaching.* Cambridge: Cambridge University Press.

Morgan, C. and Neil, P. (2001) *Teaching Modern Foreign Languages.* London: Kogan Page.

Chapter 2   Motivating pupils to learn foreign languages

AMANDA BARTON

> Without sufficient motivation, even individuals with the most remarkable abilities cannot accomplish long-term goals, and neither are appropriate curricula and good teaching enough to ensure student achievement.
>
> (Dörnyei and Csizér, 1998, p. 203)

BY THE END OF THIS CHAPTER YOU SHOULD:

- have understood that there are different kinds of motivation, and that there are a range of factors existing which influence motivation;
- have reflected on the causes of demotivation in foreign language (FL) learning;
- have a number of strategies to try out in the classroom to counter demotivation.

WHY ARE PUPILS DEMOTIVATED?

It is sad to have to confess that motivation, or the lack of it, is arguably the greatest challenge facing FL teachers in the UK. This is, of course, not at all the case in primary school when children lap up all things FLs with unabated enthusiasm and few inhibitions. In secondary school, however, there can be a shift in children's perspectives.

I would argue that pupils' attitudes to FLs play a far more important role in determining performance than they do in other subjects since the subject is not led by a factual, impersonal content, but makes particular demands on the individual. Pupils need to be especially receptive and open to internalise a foreign culture and need to have empathy with speakers of the target language (TL). Sadly, our tabloid newspapers all too often ensure that this is not the case by publishing headlines that are derogatory about our European neighbours. Headlines such as 'Huns on the run' (*Daily Sport*, April 2nd 2003) are not uncommon. Unlike our mainland European neighbours, we are unable to enjoy the benefits brought by popular music written in the TL or high levels of exposure generally to the TL(s) in our culture. In many ways, an island mentality still rules. Many pupils fail to appreciate the advantages that knowledge of a FL brings when these are not immediately evident in their everyday lives, as they are in the lives of their peers on the other side of the Channel.

Motivation is a complex construct, and in trying to unpick a range of sources researchers have identified various types. In 1972, Canadian psychologists Robert Gardner and Wallace Lambert distinguished between instrumental and integrative orientation with regard to language learning. An instrumental orientation is defined by needing to know what the value and practical applications of learning a language are, while an integrative orientation describes the desire to learn a language for its own sake, for one's own personal development and enrichment. In the broader field of motivational research these two terms are related to extrinsic motivation – where learners are motivated by the promise of external rewards, such as praise or tangible prizes – and intrinsic motivation where learners are content with the inherent satisfaction of learning.

Task 2.1

Reflecting on the causes of demotivation

Before we can begin to implement strategies to tackle demotivation, it is necessary to reflect on the causes. Thinking about pupils whom you have taught, draw up a list of the factors that influence motivation, for instance parental input and attitudes.

PARENTAL INFLUENCE

Parents' attitudes to FLs are likely to influence their children's, as the Nuffield Languages Inquiry (2000) acknowledges. In my own research, pupils often explained that their selection of one language as opposed to another had been based on a parent's viewpoint or contact with that language. The findings of the Nuffield Inquiry also suggested that parents are more likely to encourage their daughters, rather than their sons, to succeed in a language. Some research on the role played by parents has shown that socio-economic factors also make a difference; the lower the family income, the less likely parents are to support their children in learning a language (Jones, 2009). Data presented in a Government-commissioned Languages Review, conducted by Lord Dearing and Lid King, illustrates how children's attainment is directly related to their socio-economic status, based on free school meals (DFES, 2007).

Task 2.2

Parental attitudes towards FLs

Think about ways in which you might 'sell' languages to parents of children in your school, making them aware of the benefits of learning a language. Draw up your own list before reading through the list of suggested strategies below.

Suggested strategies:

- Invite parents to taster classes at school. Colleagues from other subjects could also be invited, since they also sometimes convey negative views of language learning to pupils. Alternatively, parents could be invited to join their children in language classes during an open day.

- Send home a fact sheet or quiz about the TL, including questions like: in which countries, and by how many people, is it spoken?
- Issue parents with an advice sheet on how they can help their children with their FL homework.
- Organise a languages cabaret evening or a languages open day. Pupils present short sketches both in English and the TL. Parents are served food and drink associated with countries in which the language is spoken. Local exchange associations or cultural delegations, such as the Alliance Française, Instituto Cervantes or Goethe-Institut could be invited.
- Ask ALL (Association for Language Learning, the UK's largest professional association for language teachers) for a copy of their information leaflet for parents. This outlines how languages are taught and answers the question 'Why are languages important'?

MAKING LANGUAGES RELEVANT

We should not underestimate the importance of the question 'Why do we have to learn a language?' and of receiving a valid answer. Pupils' views on whether learning a language is relevant to their own lives is widely acknowledged to be a crucial factor in creating extrinsic motivation to do well in the subject. In interviews carried out in my own research pupils in Year 8 often demonstrated an awareness of relevance as a crucial motivational factor:

> Knowing you'll use your French in the future is important. I ain't never going to use it, so there's no point in learning.
> Boy 1: … French probably wouldn't get you a job, but if you're good at maths and English…
> Boy 2: Maths and English, that's more like general knowledge, isn't it?
> Boy 3: Science … those are the sorts of things you've got to know. I don't like them, but I have to do them, that's my view.
>
> (Barton, 2006: 22)

In my research, pupils saw the benefits of learning a language largely in terms of holidays and career prospects; in line with another survey of Year 9 pupils there were very few references to the possible social and cultural advantages (Lee, Buckland and Shaw, 1998, p. 44). Pupils' perceptions of when they might use a FL were restricted to opportunities abroad; none of the pupils interviewed referred to the possibility of using a FL in the UK, a misconception which is perhaps endorsed by the predominance of overseas scenarios in the GCSE examination. The following response to the interview question, 'Do you think you will use your French in the future?' is typical of many.

> Year 7 boys:
> Boy 1: Some people might want to go on holiday, but some people don't like the French, so they won't go over.
> Boy 2: It'd be pretty useful if you like going to France.
> Boy 3: It depends. Me and S, like, we're going on the French exchange, so it'll help us there, won't it? So sometimes it can come in useful.

Task 2.3

Making FLs more real

Draw up a list of ways in which you might endeavour to make languages more real and relevant to pupils, then read through the suggested ideas below:

- Organise a trip abroad. Pupils are highly motivated by the experience of being able to use the language in an authentic context. Even a day trip to Boulogne or Aachen can make a huge difference to motivation.
- Where family income renders trips abroad impossible, organise an intensive language day. Many language colleges now organise such days, so it is worth contacting a local language college to see whether the enterprise could be shared. An intensive language day tends to involve taking all pupils in one year group off timetable and exposing them to another language for a whole day. Student teachers can be recruited to help out; the day is an invaluable experience for them, and can be particularly useful if they are given the opportunity to team teach with their peers. The school canteen could be asked to serve national foods, and pupils in other year groups could be asked to prepare labels for the foods in the TL.
- Prepare a display of advertisements that require knowledge of a FL. Pupils could be asked to bring in the adverts themselves.
- Invite in a guest speaker from business or industry to talk to pupils about how they use languages in their working life or to involve them in a project.
- A 'Languages Box' exists in some University Language Departments; this lists linguists who are prepared to go into school to talk about the applications of languages and often includes a presentation 'Why study languages?' See, for example, http://www.whystudylanguages.ac.uk/.
- Pupils prepare a presentation in which they dress up as pilots, technicians, tourist information officers, lorry drivers etc. and explain how they use languages in their jobs. The video can be shown to other classes and on Open Days in the school.
- Ensure that pupils are given sound careers guidance that does not suggest that languages are only useful if you want to become an air hostess! Pupils could take a look at the following website: http://www.prospects.ac.uk/using_your_language_skills.htm
- Tell them a joke that illustrates the usefulness of languages!
  One day, Mother Mouse spotted an open packet of biscuits lying on one of the kitchen units. As soon as the cat had gone through the kitchen cat-flap to go into the garden she ushered her baby mice across the kitchen floor. Half-way across the floor, the cat re-appeared. Quick as a flash, and using the loudest voice that she could find, Mother Mouse yelled: "Woof! Woof!" Terrified, the cat fled back into the garden. Mother Mouse then turned to her babies and said: "So, children, now you can see why it is always worth having a second language."

GENDER AND PERSONALITY

Personality, and particularly self-confidence, is an important factor in determining pupils' attitudes to learning FLs. Again, it is more of an issue in our subject since we are asking pupils to speak in front of their peers, in a language that is unfamiliar to them, at a time when they are becoming increasingly aware of the self-image they project to their peers. There seems to be some correlation between gender and self-confidence: in the interviews in my research more girls than boys expressed their dislike of speaking, but what was clear was that more assertive girls were more likely to enjoy it (Barton, 2006). It is now generally acknowledged that boys' approach to learning is often characterised by risk-taking. At Key Stage 3 they may be much more willing to risk contributing something in the TL, as girls often recognise:

> Year 8 girls:
> Girl 1: The boys are a lot more confident in speaking, I think.
> Girl 2: Because the girls always go, 'Oh, I don't know how to say it.' But the boys just say it.
> Girl 1: They just have a go and say it.
>
> (Barton, 2006: 34)

This sounds like an obvious statement, but it is all too easy to forget that FLs is often perceived as a frightening subject both by boys and girls, and that we may need to do some work on boosting pupils' confidence. Putting the department through a Japanese or Russian taster lesson at the beginning of the year or term can be a worthwhile exercise because it is an excellent reminder of how intimidating it is to be taught a language. Having staff feedback after the lesson with how they felt during the lesson – when, for instance, they were asked a question by the teacher in front of the group – can be helpful in devising strategies that are less threatening to self-aware adolescent pupils.

Task 2.4

Case study

A female Year 9 pupil appears completely unwilling to make spoken contributions in class. Write down the reasons why you think she might be unwilling to participate, together with possible steps to take to counter these, before reading the ideas below:

Reason for non-participation	Strategies

Reason for non-participation	Strategies
Embarrassment in front of peers; threat of not appearing 'cool'.	Incorporate more pair- and groupwork so that the pupil does not feel she has to perform in front of the whole class.
Fear of making a mistake in their pronunciation or accuracy.	Sensitive error correction, which does not highlight the pupil and shifts the emphasis from the individual to the whole class, i.e. whole class repeats erroneous language.
Lack of interest in the activity.	Ensure that the task has a real purpose, i.e. a genuine information gap, or has creative content.

Regardless of their greater confidence in class, much research, and attainment data, suggests that boys are far less motivated than girls to do well in learning a new language. There are numerous theories why this is the case, including: the predominance of female teaching staff which may imbue the subject with a feminine image; greater peer pressure exerted on boys than girls to underachieve; boys' greater instrumental motivation which may result in languages being perceived as less valuable if the practical applications are left unhighlighted; and boys' lack of interest generally in communication skills. Much research has now been conducted in this field (see, for instance, Polat, 2011; McCall, 2011; Kissau, 2006; Carr and Pauwels, 2006). The gender gap in secondary school remains an area of concern for Government, and FLs is one of those subjects where the gap remains at its greatest.

SUMMARY

While our pupils continue to see the world as a largely Anglophone environment in which the need to learn other languages is relegated to inferior status, motivating children in the FLs classroom will continue to pose a challenge for many teachers. The provision of FLs in the primary school, as well as its inclusion in the so-called English Baccalaureate, may, however, go some way to promoting its status both inside the classroom and in society in general. In the meantime, it falls to the teacher not just to teach languages, but to sell the subject to their pupils as the life-enhancing experience which we recognise it to be.

REFERENCES

Barton, A. (2006) *Getting the Buggers into Languages*. 2nd edition. London: Continuum.

Carr, J. and Pauwels, A. (2006) *Boys and Foreign Language Learning: Real Boys don't do Languages*. New York: Palgrave MacMillan.

DfES (Department for Education and Skills) (2007) *Languages Review*. London.

Dörnyei, Z. and Csizér, K. (1998) 'Ten Commandments for motivating language learners: results of an empirical study'. *Language Teaching Research*, 2(3), 203–224.

Jones, C. (2009) 'Parental support and the attitudes of boys and girls to modern foreign languages'. *Language Learning Journal*, 37(1), 85–97.

Kissau, S. (2006) 'Gender differences in motivation to learn French'. *Canadian Modern Language Review*, 62(3), 401–422.

Lee, J., Buckland, D. and Shaw, G. (1998) *The Invisible Child*. London: CILT.

McCall, I. (2011) 'Score in French: motivating boys with football in Key Stage 3'. *Language Learning Journal*, 39(1), 5–18.

Nuffield Foundation (2000) *Languages: The Next Generation.* The Final Report and Recommendations of the Nuffield Languages Inquiry. London: Nuffield Foundation.

Polat, N. (2011) 'Gender differences in motivation and L2 accent attainment: an investigation of young Kurdish learners of Turkish'. *Language Learning Journal*, 39(1), 19–41.

Chapter 3   Presenting new vocabulary and structures

SUE FIELD

BY THE END OF THIS CHAPTER YOU SHOULD:

- recognise the need to teach new vocabulary/structures;
- have an appreciation of the process of selecting key lexical items to stimulate topic-based foreign language (FL) learning;
- be aware of the range of resources available, particularly visual aids;
- be able to draw on a bank of FL presentation activities to sequence and structure the learning experience.

KNOWLEDGE UNDERPINNING THE TEACHING OF NEW VOCABULARY AND STRUCTURES

Assimilating vocabulary/structures is an essential part of language learning. Meaning cannot be conveyed without vocabulary. Examination specifications demand that pupils acquire a vocabulary of up to 2,000 words, as well as structures and collocations (i.e. words which 'belong together', e.g. *Sport treiben*). Some vocabulary is for passive use, but the majority is for active. At Advanced level, there is no defined list of lexical items; the range of vocabulary is vast.

Vocabulary can be defined as single words, easily translatable from one language to another. Cognates (words which can transfer between languages, e.g. *radio*) present little challenge for learners. Some words contain clues to meaning, such as compound nouns and separable verbs in German, or have common stems (e.g. *verdier*). Structures, e.g. *ich möchte*, carry meaning or purpose, providing utterances with a force (requests, negatives, questions, imperatives, etc.). Concepts, consisting of combinations of words, are not directly translatable, often requiring an appreciation of cultural contexts for a full understanding.

Although vocabulary/structures are acquired incidentally throughout learning, this chapter looks at ways in which the teacher overtly facilitates the process of vocabulary learning. Notwithstanding a developing focus on content and integrated learning (CLIL), 'Presentation-Practice-Production' (PPP) is traditional within communicative language teaching (CLT) (see e.g. *Learning to Teach FLs in the Secondary School*, fourth edition, Routledge, Chapter 5). It demands that, within individual lessons and throughout a series of lessons, pupils:

1   are presented sets of language forms;
2   are given opportunities to practise;

3   manipulate language for their own purposes.

The presentation stage is not only significant in terms of its position in the sequence (i.e. to engage pupils' interest from the start of the lesson), but also provides essential elements enabling pupils to participate in subsequent activities and meet specified learning outcomes.

First, learners recognise the sight and sound of the word, identified by Grauberg (1997) as 'discrimination', before moving on to 'understanding meaning'. If pupils relate the word/structure to a concept, rather than to a translation, they begin to commit this to long-term memory by connecting this to a (mental) image, sound, movement, event or process. Pupils' preferred learning styles will determine the efficacy of each of these for themselves; the first three would appeal respectively to visual, auditory and kinaesthetic learners.

WHICH VOCABULARY AND STRUCTURES, AND HOW MANY FOR EACH LESSON?

Decisions will be based upon the scheme of work, which normally relates to a text book, examination specifications and the National Curriculum Programme of Study, etc. The teacher exercises professional judgement in selecting the most useful lexical items.

Context

What are the lexical items required for this particular topic/unit, and how can this vocabulary be broken down into individual lessons?

For example, within a unit on 'Around town', directions and types of shops may be presented in separate lessons, and then learnt in combination. Key words could be *links, rechts, geradeaus*; a key structure could be *Nimm die erste Strasse…*

Intended learning outcomes

What should pupils be able to do with the vocabulary by the end of the lesson, and why?

Teachers must clarify whether the language is for receptive or productive use. This helps the teacher to identify key structures; for example, imperatives, questions and negatives.

Prior learning

What have pupils already learnt?

Activities enabling pupils to recall known vocabulary/structures, and to build upon them, must be considered.

Complexity of lexical items or concepts

Are these hard or easy to understand or pronounce? How many words can pupils be expected to learn, and which are for receptive or productive use?

Pupil characteristics

What is the ability range and motivation of the class? Are they beginner, intermediate or advanced learners?

Time

When does the lesson take place? How long is the lesson? These influence pupil motivation, and the quantity of new language pupils will be able to assimilate.

Task 3.1

Vocabulary and structures

Choose one unit from the former QCA scheme of work for Key Stage 3 French, German or Spanish (archived at http://webarchive.nationalarchives.gov.uk/20090 608182316/http://standards.dfes.gov.uk/schemes2/) to work with for these tasks.

A   From reading *all* of the information given within the unit of work, devise a list of vocabulary and structures which would be appropriate. Identify which are for receptive and which are for productive use. (The units are, broadly speaking, sequential, so Units 1–6 are intended for Year 7, and so on.)

Vocabulary and structures	
Productive	Receptive

B   Extract the pupil learning outcomes from the unit. Consider how these lexical items contribute to each of these. Divide the list of vocabulary and structures into categories appropriate for each of the learning outcomes. Within each of these categories, grade the lexical items from simple to complex.

Pupil learning outcomes	Vocabulary and structures (from simple to complex)

C   Consider how these learning outcomes might be broken down further, and re-combined into intended learning outcomes for individual lessons. Sequence these into ten lessons of one hour's duration for a class of average ability. What new lexical items would be presented in each lesson? How might you alter this for a class of low or high ability? (Consider the differentiated 'Expectations' outlined for the unit.)

	Pupil Learning Outcomes	Vocabulary and structures
Lesson 1	- -	
Differentiation		
...		

WHICH RESOURCES TO USE?

Choosing resources for presenting language is important. For learners at Key Stages 4 and at post 16, this may take the form of a text (spoken or written), from which pupils extrapolate new lexical items. Tapes, CDs and a variety of reading materials serve as resources here.

For all pupils, visual aids provide an effective way to focus and engage interest, and to establish concepts. In this way, the status of the TL is enhanced at a crucial stage of the learning process. Visual aids are not only used to represent items at face value (e.g. nouns), but also to represent qualities (e.g. adjectives), as well as to symbolise longer structures (e.g. *Il n'y a pas de quoi*). Such structures (and, therefore, the same visual aids) may be used in different units, allowing for the transferability of knowledge and skills.

In choosing the visual aids, important questions are:

- Are they appropriate for the particular topic?
- Do they enable learners to use language in a quasi-authentic way?
- Will they 'grab' pupils' attention? Are they attractive, not out-dated, and of interest?
- Will they encourage pupils to link meaning and concepts?
- How flexible are they? Can they be used in subsequent activities and units?
- Is the time required to prepare them well spent?

A range of resources is available to teachers, which enables the accommodation of all learning styles over a period of time.

Flashcards	Very versatile, can be handled by pupils.
Interactive whiteboard (IWB)	Has all the advantages of a computer screen on display to all pupils, with the added advantages of touch-screen facilities. A range of software, such as Task Magic (http://mdlsoft.co.uk) and Storybird (http://storybird.com), is available to be used with the IWB.
PowerPoint	Can be used as 'virtual flashcards' (which can also be printed off for further use). Animation enables sound and movement to be added, as well as overlaying words. Composite pictures can be produced.
Video/CD Rom/DVD	Combines sound (commentary) and moving image; can be 'frozen' to provide still visuals.
Visualisers	A multi-media system which combines many of the above. It has the added advantage of projecting actual items onto a screen, rather than as silhouettes.
Display (including labels)	Links concepts and images through forms of labelling. This encourages passive learning of vocabulary, as well as developing cultural awareness.
Human resources	Voice, mime, movement, expressions, gestures, obeying commands (imperatives). These add an authentic human touch. Also personal attributes, clothes, etc. – but needs sensitive handling.
Realia	Authentic items from the country where the TL is spoken. Provide opportunities for developing cultural awareness. Realia can be used and handled in an authentic way.
Props	Cross-cultural artefacts. Can be handled by the pupils.
Whiteboard	Replacement screen display area for combining written words and symbols, enabling the teacher to interact with pupils. Good for visual representation of a time-line, for tenses.
Overhead projector (OHP)	Although becoming less common in classrooms, can still be used to project pictures, words, symbols, silhouettes of objects on to a screen. On/off switch and focus button can be used to good effect. Possibility of presenting images in reverse.

Figure 3.1 Resources for presenting language

Task 3.2

Matching resources to lexical items

Using the outcomes of Task 3.1, the aim of this activity is to match appropriate resources to the new lexical items to be taught and learnt.

A   Consider which of the resources identified within the chapter would be most effective in presenting the particular lexical items. The teacher needs to be aware of the 'force' of the new structures (requests, negatives, questions, imperatives, etc.) in order to match this with appropriate resources.

Vocabulary and structures	Language force	Resource

B   Comment on the qualities of the particular resources you have identified, with reference to the list of important questions when choosing visual aids.

	Resource 1	Resource 2	Resource 3
Appropriateness to topic?			
Quasi-authenticity?			
Attention 'grabbing'?			
Conceptual linking?			
Flexibility?			
Preparation worthwhile?			

C   Do the activities you have identified reflect a bias towards one particular learning style; for example visual or auditory learners? What do you need to do to balance this in your teaching? Discuss with your mentor the type of activities and resources she uses for particular topics. Can you think of ways to broaden your repertoire?

WHICH ACTIVITIES CAN BE INCLUDED IN THE PRESENTATION PHASE?

Harris and Snow (2004) suggest one must hear a word 12 times before it can be remembered, and, therefore, repeated exposure is required. This process relies on teacher input, although pupils must be given opportunities to use the language meaningfully, through multi-sensory activities. These need to be sequenced, allowing pupils to gain confidence. Attention should be paid to pace and transitions.

Phased activities include the following:

Listening activities

Pupils listen attentively, whilst given the opportunity to internalise new sounds.

- *Guessing what new words might be*
  Provide a stimulus for active listening; for example, a picture on the board. Items for use could be revealed slowly, providing clues to the topic area, such as clothes in a suitcase. The keyhole technique with OHP (a hole cut out of a piece of paper, moved across the transparency), or with the IWB, can be used in the same way.
- *Identifying new words within a text*
  Circling new or key vocabulary within a text, either from a written or spoken stimulus.
- *Odd one out*
  For aural acuity purposes; pupils pick from three utterances (e.g. *les yeux verts, les yeux gris, les yeux verts*).

Listening and repeating activities

Pupils need to be encouraged to repeat after a model, practising pronunciation of new vocabulary/structures – as a whole class, as smaller groups, and, finally, individually. Large groups of pupils can be resistant to choral repetition exercises, so imaginative ways to encourage pupils to take part should be deployed:

- vary the tone and style of voice;
- introduce an element of competition (one side of the room versus the other);
- hum, chant or clap to a rhythm (e.g. rap);
- build up phrases backwards (this is particularly useful as a way of building up to longer structures);
- repeat if it's true (see Buckby, 1980).

For 'repeat if it's true', pupils repeat a word or phrase only if it corresponds to the visual aid being presented at the time. Conducted as a game, it enables pupils to demonstrate what they have remembered from the initial presentation in a non-threatening climate. This moves pupils towards linking sound and image to meaning. Teachers can monitor progress on a whole-class basis, and it also encourages pupils to listen actively to new vocabulary.

Matching activities

Pupils can demonstrate on an individual basis whether or not they are making the required links to meaning. They may not generate language themselves, but they must make choices based on whether the sound and image match.

- *Pupils match images to words*
  Touching or pointing at a visual aid, or by referring to a number or name.
- *Miming, including pantomime competitions*
  Individuals or groups of pupils mime a word or action, either in response to a stimulus, or for others to speculate as to the meaning.

Question and answer activities

Questioning needs to be graded in order to build pupils' confidence and follow the 'hierarchy of questions':

1. *Closed questions*, requiring yes/no or true/false responses demand receptive knowledge of the language (similar to matching activities).
2. *Alternative questions* require pupils to choose between two utterances and to reproduce this language. Although a closed question, it has the benefit of allowing pupils to repeat after a model.
3. *Target or goal questions* are open, and correct answers reveal a productive knowledge of new vocabulary/structures, and a readiness to move on to the practice stage.
   - *Noughts and crosses*
     Flashcards stuck onto the whiteboard (3x3) or the IWB can be used for this. Pupils nominate a particular space on the grid for their team by correctly identifying the image within it (i.e. by providing the answer to the target question). (As pupils have a choice of up to nine utterances, they can 'get away with' not yet knowing the full list of new lexical items; see also guessing activities below.)

Guessing games

There is a range of activities which require pupils to make guesses as to the 'identity' of an item of vocabulary. This is a way of getting the pupils to produce language for themselves; it allows pupils to offer answers to open questions, even if they are not sure of the entire list of new vocabulary. Again, getting a 'wrong' answer is not threatening; it simply demonstrates they have guessed incorrectly. It provides a chance for the teacher to monitor individual pupils' progress.

- *Blind man's buff*
  Individual pupils close their eyes, and are asked to point at images (most probably flashcards/posters) located around the room. When used for places in a town, this allows for authentic interaction (e.g. *'Où est la gare?'*, *'La gare est là-bas.'*).
- *Play your cards right*
  Visual aids are concealed one at a time (e.g. flashcards reversed), and the class have to guess the identity of each in turn. This is effective if played as a team game.
- *Blockbusters*
  Pupils guess the vocabulary/structures from initials on a grid. Also relies on memory (see below).

Memory games

Learners are given opportunities to commit items to long-term memory.

- *Kim's game*
  Visual aids are displayed; one is removed; pupils have to identify which one. PowerPoint, IWB and the OHP can be used here.
- *I went to market*
  Pupils take turns to add to the list of new lexical items, which have to be remembered and repeated in order within a sentence. This works well with shopping vocabulary, and the structure *J'ai acheté/ich habe…gekauft*, but should not be restricted to this topic.

- *Conveyor belt (as in The Generation Game)*
  A series of images is moved across the screen (PowerPoint, IWB, or on an OHP transparency), and pupils work in teams to remember as many as possible (see Harris *et al.*, 2001).
- *Who wants to be a millionaire?*
  Computer software is available for this, although it can also be played using cards.

Interaction activities

Opportunities need to be created for pupil:pupil as well as teacher:pupil interaction.

- *Distributing visual aids*
  Pupils ask for items using structures presented. If they then conceal these, others can be charged with the task of recovering them by using the appropriate language.
- *Pupils as teacher*
  When sufficiently confident about new language, pupils may act as the teacher by working on the IWB, or manipulating the flashcards, for the benefit of the class.

Task 3.3

Sequencing activities at the presentation stage

Using the outcomes of Tasks 3.1 and 3.2, the aim of this activity is to sequence the activities at the presentation stage of the lessons.

A Describe the activities which would be possible with the resources, and why these would maximise their potential effectiveness.

Resource	Activity	Rationale (pupil motivation, etc.)

B Organise the list of activities above into an appropriate sequence, with reference to the phases in presenting new language identified in the chapter. Consider teacher and pupil TL use, including teacher questions and prompts, in each of these phases.

Phase	Activity	TL use	
		Teacher	Pupil
Listening			
Repeating			
Matching			

Phase	Activity	TL use	
		Teacher	Pupil
Q & A			
Guessing			
Memory			
Interaction			

C   Discuss with your mentor how she recognises when pupils are ready to move on to the next phase of the presentation stage. What are the signs, and how can this monitoring be incorporated into the teaching and learning activities?

SUMMARY

When presenting new vocabulary and structures, activities organised by the teacher should be underpinned by knowledge of what is 'learnable', and at what stages of learning particular activities have the greatest impact. The teacher has a wide range of resources available, and, therefore, decisions on which resources are most suited to each topic, as well as to each activity, must be made.

USEFUL WEBSITES

Internet Picture Dictionary
http://www.pdictionary.com

Language Guide
http://www.languageguide.org

Education Scotland MFL
http://www.educationscotland.gov.uk/learningteachingandassessment/curriculum
    areas/languages/modernlanguages/supportmaterials/

The Ashcombe School
http://www.ashcombe.surrey.sch.uk/legacy/Curriculum/mod lang/index_teaching.htm

REFERENCES

Buckby, M. (1980) *Action! Book 1*. Sunbury-on-Thames: Nelson.
Grauberg, W. (1997) *The Elements of Foreign Language Teaching*. Clevedon: Multilingual Matters.
Harris, V., Burch, J., Jones, B. and Darcy, J. (2001) *Something to Say*. London: CILT.
Harris, V. and Snow, D. (2004) *Doing it for Themselves*. London: CILT.
Pachler, N., Evans, M., Redondo, A. and Fisher, L. (2014) *Learning to Teach Foreign Languages in the Secondary School*. 4th edition. London: Routledge.

Chapter 4   Developing foreign language skills through formative assessment

TREVOR MUTTON

BY THE END OF THIS CHAPTER YOU SHOULD:

- understand the purposes of different techniques for assessment used in the foreign language (FL) classroom;
- be aware of a range of strategies and techniques for carrying out formative assessment;
- be aware of the ways in which feedback can be given to learners; and
- have an understanding of the potential benefits and some of the issues involved in using formative assessment in the FL classroom.

WHY IS ASSESSMENT SUCH AN IMPORTANT ISSUE?

Assessment enables us, as teachers, to evaluate the effectiveness of our planning and teaching but, properly implemented, allows us also to do so much more in that it provides us (and our pupils) with the evidence needed to inform further learning and ongoing language development. The Teachers' Standards for England (Department for Education, 2011) state that all teachers have to be able to '(m)ake accurate and productive use of assessment' which includes being able to 'make use of formative and summative assessment to secure pupils' progress' (Standard 6), and assessment for learning approaches are now firmly embedded in the practice of the majority of schools. It is important, however, that we understand as fully as possible both the principles underpinning effective approaches to assessment in the FLs classroom as well as the relationship between these practices and effective teaching and learning more generally.

WHY DO WE ASSESS PUPILS?

There are a number of reasons why teachers need to assess pupils and these fall broadly into the following categories (see also Pachler, Evans, Redondo and Fisher, 2014):

- to determine the extent to which the learning objectives for any lesson/series of lessons have been met;
- to evaluate how effective specific teaching strategies may have been in bringing about the desired learning;

- to identify what pupils may need to do next in order to develop their learning further;
- to measure performance in relation to other pupils, or in relation to a specific set of criteria;
- to gain external accreditation;
- to predict how pupils may perform (e.g. in external examinations);
- to provide data that will contribute to judgements about the overall effectiveness of teaching and learning within a school;
- to provide the information needed to report on the progress of individual students to others (e.g. parents and carers);
- as a tool for increasing motivation; and
- to inform decisions as to which teaching groups pupils may be placed in.

FORMATIVE AND SUMMATIVE ASSESSMENT

The above purposes could be seen to fall into one of two categories – they could be said to be either **summative** or **formative** in nature.

Summative assessment is used when a teacher makes a judgement about how well a pupil is performing, often against a set of specific criteria (e.g. grade-related criteria). The information obtained from summative assessments is often shared with others and may be used to assign a grade or level to pupils, to relate the achievement to national standards, to provide a record of progress over time, to make comparisons in relation to performance across a range of subjects in the school etc. For this reason the assessment carried out needs to be both valid (i.e. it actually measures what it intends to measure) and reliable (i.e. it is accurate and consistent). Summative assessment is often referred to as assessment *of* learning, but that is not to say that summative assessment may not also be used for formative purposes.

Formative assessment is defined by Black and Wiliam (1998) as referring to:

> all those activities undertaken by teachers *and by their students in assessing themselves,* which provide information to be used as feedback to modify the teaching and learning activities in which they are engaged. *Such assessment becomes 'formative assessment' when the evidence is actually used to adapt the teaching work to meet student needs.*

Formative assessment is now frequently referred to as 'assessment *for* learning' (or AfL) and is used primarily as a diagnostic tool within the classroom. It has been defined by the Assessment Reform Group (2002) as:

> the process of seeking and interpreting evidence for use by learners and their teachers to decide where the learners are in their learning, where they need to go and how best to get there.

This group has also defined the key principles that characterise formative assessment in the classroom and state that assessment for learning should:

- be part of effective planning of teaching and learning;
- focus on how students learn;
- be recognised as central to classroom practice;
- be regarded as a key to professional skill for teachers;

- be sensitive and constructive because any assessment has an emotional impact;
- take account of the importance of learner motivation;
- promote commitment to learning goals and a shared understanding of the criteria by which they are assessed;
- enable learners to receive constructive guidance about how to improve;
- develop learners' capacity for self-assessment so that they can become reflective and self-managing; and
- recognise the full range of achievements of all learners.

Formative assessment is, therefore, an integral part of teaching and learning and is an ongoing process in the classroom, but it is important to consider carefully the purposes of any assessment that is carried out and the way in which the evidence that results from such assessments is used in order to promote pupil learning. In a detailed analysis of the nature of assessment for learning, Wiliam (2011) emphasises this in the following way:

> Two features appear to be particularly important in designing assessment that will support learning. One is that the evidence ... is more than information about the presence of a gap between current and desired performance. The evidence must also provide information about what kinds of instructional activities are likely to result in improving performance. ... The second requirement is that the learner engages in actions to improve learning; this may be undertaking the remedial activities provided by the teacher, asking a peer for specific help, or reflecting on different ways to move her own learning forward—after all, the best designed feedback is useless if it is not acted upon.
>
> (Wiliam, 2011)

Task 4.1

Purposes and types of assessment tasks

Below you will find a list of some assessment tasks that might be carried out in the FLs classroom. Firstly, identify what you think the main *purpose* of each of the assessments might be and then decide whether this is an example of *formative* or *summative* assessment. Then consider the ways in which any evidence collected might be further used by the teacher, or by the pupils themselves, to develop pupil learning.

Do any of these activities raise issues about what is actually being assessed and for what purpose?

For those that you identify as being primarily summative in nature discuss how these might also, where possible, be further used in relation to a formative dimension.

Assessment activity	Purpose	Formative or summative?	Examples of the way in which the evidence from the assessment might be used by teachers and/or pupils to develop learning further
Assessing individuals who are involved in a pair work oral activity in which they are discussing likes and dislikes of foods.			
Assessing a reading task in which pupils have to look at a brochure and then respond to true/ false statements in relation to the facilities in a town.			
Assessing a dialogue/ short scene in a café where pupils are working as a group and assigning a level to the performance of individuals.			
Monitoring pupil responses to teacher-led questions about family and pets in a whole class setting.			
A plenary task that involves pupils feeding back on what they have learnt about asking and giving directions.			
Collecting in the marks following a listening exercise in which pupils had to identify the hobbies of a group of native speakers on tape.			
A 'whiteboard' activity that involves pupils indicating whether a statement that the teacher has read out is true or false.			

Assessment activity	Purpose	Formative or summative?	Examples of the way in which the evidence from the assessment might be used by teachers and/or pupils to develop learning further
A vocabulary test, focusing on 10 items of clothing.			
Assessing a piece of writing in which pupils talk about their school.			
Feedback on a written piece, completed as homework, about what the pupil did last weekend.			
An end of unit test covering all aspects of the topic 'House and Home'.			
A GCSE listening test that is carried out as a practice activity in class.			
An essay related to the issue of young people in the target country.			
A discussion with colleagues following an analysis of the 'end of module' test scores for the entire Year 8 cohort.			

INTEGRATING FORMATIVE ASSESSMENT INTO PLANNING

The opportunities to carry out effective formative assessment cannot just be left to chance – they need careful planning and should be integrated into the whole process of teaching and learning (see also Chapter 2). Lesson planning will demonstrate this in a number of ways but primarily it will take into account an evaluation of the most recent teaching and learning experiences with the pupils in question, drawing on a range of available evidence (i.e. any informal or formal assessment carried out in previous lessons and reflection on this), as well as the assessment opportunities that need to be integrated into subsequent lessons for the cycle to continue. A key aspect of this is the identification of appropriate learning objectives and the planning of specific learning outcomes, but even these will then need to be broken up into smaller steps in learning (the constituent parts of any lesson plan) and for each of these smaller steps the teacher will have to make a judgement as to what extent the learning within each of these smaller steps has been met. This judgement might be as the result of informal monitoring of pupil responses (e.g. gauging the accuracy of pupil responses during a question and answer session as part of the presentation phase of the lesson in which new vocabulary is being introduced) but in other cases be more structured (e.g. assessing the work produced from a reading exercise). In both cases the information gained will be used to inform the teacher of a number of things, for example:

- the extent to which the learning objectives have or have not been met;
- the action that may need to be taken by the teacher to address any issues arising from this analysis;
- the feedback that may need to be given to individual pupils to inform them of specific aspects of their learning (see below);
- the action that pupils (individuals or their peers) may need to take in order to further their learning.

Task 4.2

Linking assessment to learning objectives

Focus on a lesson/series of lessons that you are soon to teach and plan in detail the way in which you will assess the learning that you want to take place. Think about how you will assess each of the micro objectives, as well as the overall learning objectives in order to get a clearer picture of what the pupils have actually learnt. It might be helpful to identify the overall learning objectives first, and then the smaller steps (the micro objectives) that will lead to the planned learning taking place, then the activities that you might use to bring about the learning and finally how the learning will be assessed.

Example:
Topic: House and Home

Learning objectives:
Pupils will know the names of the rooms in the house and be able to describe what rooms they have in their own house.

Micro-objective	Activity	Assessment opportunities
Revision of previous work	Game to revise 'à la campagne', 'en ville' etc.	Monitoring pupil contributions
Become familiar with the sounds of the new vocabulary	Introduce new language using PowerPoint presentation	Informal monitoring of receptivity
Practise pronunciation	Repetition and question and answer sequence	Informal monitoring of responses

etc.

and later in the lesson:

Use the new language in a structured dialogue	Group work activity, with pupils working in threes to carry out dialogues in pairs using questions and answers to ascertain details of where the other lives	Teacher: monitoring to assess recall of vocabulary and accuracy of pronunciation Peer assessment: one pupil in the group (in turn) to monitor and assess the responses
Use the new language independently	Written activity – using a writing frame to generate pupils account of their own house/flat etc.	Assessment of written work and in-depth feedback comments

SELF-ASSESSMENT AND PEER-ASSESSMENT

Self-assessment and peer-assessment should be seen as valuable tools in the classroom and ones that can have an impact on the way that pupils learn as part of the overall framework of formative assessment in the FLs classroom. This can be achieved through increased levels of learner autonomy, through collaborative learning (since pupils are discussing together specific aspects of their work and providing the opportunity to learn from each other through feedback) and through pupils being able to reflect on and share specific learning strategies.

However, the integration of self-assessment and peer-assessment is not a straightforward matter and depends on pupils being equipped with the necessary understanding and skills to carry out such activities effectively. These will include:

- a knowledge of the learning goals towards which they have been working;
- an understanding of the criteria by which the assessments are being carried out;
- a model in their heads of what a good piece of work might look like;
- practice in applying criteria to specific pieces of work; and
- the ability to give positive feedback to help the other learner develop.

The teacher will clearly need to make the learning goals and the criteria explicit as well as modelling how the self-assessment and peer-assessment process might work. The skills can be taught gradually, through practice, once the initial expectation of working in this way has been established. As Black and Jones (2006) state:

Our work with teachers has shown that peer assessment helps pupils develop their self-assessment skills. Pupils can be taught to recognise both quality and inadequacies in other pupils' work even if their own level of competence is different from the level of the work that they are reading. With coaching focussed on criteria for quality, pupils can develop awareness of successes and problems in pieces of work and can articulate this in discussion, a process which teachers can help by providing regular comments to serve as models. As pupils assimilate the criteria, they thereby assess their own work with greater clarity. Such practice encourages improvement as pupils begin to see how small changes, or different ways of approaching parts of the work, can easily raise its quality – and the regular small pushes forward help embed better learning and raise overall attainment.

(Black and Jones, 2006)

The following are suggestions as to how peer-assessment activities might be approached in relation to specific FLs activities, but all depend to some extent on the pupils having the knowledge, understanding and skills as described above.

Speaking activities

- asking the class to assess oral presentations that groups of pupils, or individuals, have produced;
- asking pupils to devise their own criteria for assessing an oral performance, based on their understanding of the learning goals, and then asking them to apply these;
- asking pupils to assess each other in groups of three; two pupils will perform a pair work task and the other pupil will carry out an assessment of one or both of the others, perhaps recording the results on a sheet (see also Pachler, Evans, Redondo and Fisher, 2014, Chapter 15);
- as above, but one pupil will give a short presentation to the other two, who will assess the performance and then discuss the results together.

Writing activities

- before you ask pupils to write a particular piece, provide an example with anticipated errors in it that pupils correct individually, or in pairs, providing as they do so reasons for their choices;
- give group feedback by using a text you have written that contains the most common errors that pupils have made and correct as above;
- produce a list of words in pairs, with a correct and an incorrect version (based on errors that pupils may have made) and correct as above;
- allow pupils to discuss a piece of completed work before it is handed in to see if one pupil could discover any errors in another pupil's work and vice-versa.

Reading and listening activities

- pupils review their work together after it is completed and discuss where any improvements could be made;
- pupils discuss together what they have found difficult/straightforward in the task and provide feedback to you (possibly using 'traffic lighting');
- pupils discuss together what strategies they have used in dealing with the text in question.

Task 4.3

Self- and peer-assessment

Using some of the activities from Task 4.1 again, this time identify how each of these assessment opportunities might be developed in order to incorporate peer-assessment and/or self-assessment in a meaningful and productive way.

Discuss any of the issues that arise from taking such an approach and how these might be successfully addressed.

Assessment activity	Use of peer-assessment /self-assessment
Assessing individuals who are involved in a pair work oral activity in which they are discussing likes and dislikes of foods.	
Assessing a reading task in which pupils have to look at a brochure and then respond to true/false statements in relation to the facilities in a town.	
Assessing a dialogue/short scene in a café where pupils are working as a group and assigning a level to the performance of individuals.	
Monitoring pupil responses to teacher led questions about family and pets in a whole class setting.	
A plenary task that involves pupils feeding back on what they have learnt about asking and giving directions.	
Collecting in the marks following a listening exercise in which pupils had to identify the hobbies of a group of native speakers on tape.	
A vocabulary test, focusing on 10 items of clothing	
Assessing a piece of writing in which pupils talk about their school.	
Feedback on a written piece, completed as homework, about what the pupil did last weekend.	
An end of unit test covering all aspects of the topic 'House and Home'.	
A GCSE listening test that is carried out as a practice activity in class.	
An essay related to the issue of young people in the target country.	

Now look at the Scheme of Work or your own medium-term plans for a unit of work that you will soon be teaching and identify specific activities where peer or self-assessment might be incorporated, and the precise ways in which you see this working.

GIVING FEEDBACK TO PUPILS FOR WRITING

Teachers spend a significant amount of time assessing pupils' work and marking is often seen as time-consuming, so it is important that assessment of pupil work is done as effectively as possible. Whilst some assessment will, by its nature, be more summative than formative (e.g. marking end of unit assessments), a lot of what the teacher does can be categorised as the latter and be seen as assessment *for* learning (as opposed to assessment *of* learning). This can contribute to the pupils' development of their language skills in two ways – firstly the teacher will use the information gained from assessing the work to inform future planning that will take into account what pupils have learnt and what they still need to learn; and secondly it will enable the teacher to give *individualised* feedback to pupils. Clearly there is not time to provide in-depth individualised feedback on each piece of work that the pupil produces but it should, however, be possible to use a range of assessment strategies according to the nature of the task being assessed, the purposes of the assessment etc.

It may be useful to consider two levels of assessment:

1   *overview assessments*, which might entail the following:
    • a check that the activity has been completed;
    • a snapshot impression as to whether the learning objectives have been met and to what extent planning needs to be amended in the light of the pupils' performance on the task;
    • a brief analysis of how the pupil has performed;
    • a brief analysis of any areas that need further development;
    • brief feedback.
2   *in-depth assessments*, which would be characterised by:
    • a more detailed analysis of the strengths of the piece of work;
    • an analysis of the key areas for development;
    • full written feedback that provides details of the strengths of the piece, one or two specific areas that the pupil might need to work on as a result of the feedback, and suggestions as to how the pupil might achieve this improvement (including suggestions for learning strategies);
    • the facilitation of a dialogue between pupil and teacher, with the teacher possibly asking questions to which the pupil subsequently responds (e.g. 'What do you have to remember about the past participle in a German sentence?');
    • a limited number of 'targeted' errors being highlighted, all of which relate to the learning point on which the teacher is focusing.

Task 4.4

Assessing writing

Look at the piece of work below from a Year 10 pupil (the task was to describe a recent holiday).

How would you go about assessing this piece of work in a way that would place the emphasis on the principles of formative assessment?

What would you highlight as being strengths of the piece? What specific error(s) would you decide to focus on? Precisely what in-depth feedback would you give?

If you discovered that some of the errors are characteristic of the work of a number of pupils in the class how might you approach the issues when giving general feedback to the class, or adapt the next stage of your teaching to take into account this information?

Account of a holiday

L'année dernière ma famille et me suis allé à l'Italie sur les vacances pour deux semaines, nous sommes restés dans une villa avec sa proper piscine, la villa était stupéfiante et il avait une belle vue des montagnes, c'était trés chaud et ensoleillé pour le premièrement coupler de jours que nous venons de relâcher et sommes allès nager, sur la deuxième samaine nous avons loué une voiture et avons conduit environ visitant des villes, pendant les vacances nous avons dépensé beaucoup de temps commercial et nageant c'était grand! A l'avenir j'aimerais rentrer à l'Italie parce que c'est stupéfaint, il faisait chaud et j àvais un vraiment bon temps.

GIVING FEEDBACK IN RELATION TO THE OTHER LANGUAGE LEARNING SKILLS

Whilst it is relatively easy to incorporate formative feedback into one's assessment practices in relation to writing tasks, it is perhaps less straightforward when it comes to the other language skills.

Speaking

The majority of feedback given in relation to speaking tasks tends to be immediate and given verbally, often focused on the correction of errors in accuracy or pronunciation (see below). It is however worth considering the possibility of giving feedback for the pupils' speaking performance in *writing* from time to time; pupils who receive such feedback tend to value it and to use it as a real focus for developing their learning since they have time to digest it fully, reflect on what needs to be done and go back to it if necessary.

There are, however, clearly some issues that have to be addressed when considering how to make full use of oral assessments in order to promote learning in the classroom.

<table>
<tr><td colspan="2">Task 4.5</td></tr>
<tr><td colspan="2">

Assessing oral work

What are the issues that might constrain the effective use of assessing oral work in the classroom? In what ways might these be addressed? Add to the list below and suggest solutions that might facilitate such assessment.

</td></tr>
</table>

Issue	What can be done?
It is impossible to get round all the pupils in one lesson	Spread the assessments over a period of time – aim for one 'in-depth assessment per pupil for each unit of work
The assessment will not be valid if individual pupils are assessed at different times and at different stages of the unit	It doesn't matter since the purpose of the assessment is *not to provide summative data but to develop the learning of the individual pupil* through the assessment and feedback process
Other pupils may need my help whilst I am trying to assess two pupils involved in a pair work task	
others?	

Listening and reading

It appears to be fairly common practice in some FLs classrooms to carry out a listening activity that involves the pupils recording their responses in some way (completing a grid; indicating true/false phrases etc.) and then for the teacher to go through the exercise and get the pupils to 'mark' their work. At the end the results may be collected in, or a show of hands indicates the pupils who got 8, 7, 6 etc. items correct. Such assessment data gives little information. If an individual pupil gets a mark of 4 out of a possible 6, for example, this does not tell the teacher which two items the pupil had difficulty with, or whether all the pupils who achieved the same mark had difficulty with the same two items. Although some course books may attach levels to tasks, the collection of marks alone fails to give any qualitative information that might inform future teaching and learning.

Rather than assessing all listening (or reading) activities in a similar way, it would be preferable to plan which tasks in these skills will be designated as assessment activities from which you gain appropriate information about the learning process. It is not easy to give detailed feedback in relation to these skills, but it is nevertheless possible, and the following might be ways of achieving this:

- monitor a number of individual pupils whilst they are doing listening or reading exercise and note the ways in which they are working;
- collect in the work that is produced and analyse what they seem to do well/ less well;

- focus on the use of learner strategies – get pupils to tell you how they approach tasks and the strategies they use and relate feedback to their apparent effectiveness;
- get pupils to comment on their own performance in writing after the task has been completed and respond to these comments.

Task 4.6

Assessing listening and reading

Fill in the table below, identifying the different types of assessment for listening (L) and reading (R) activities that you could use. In each case identify which skill the activity relates to and then think about what the pupils are being required to do in order for you to assess their level of comprehension. Which are well-suited (or less well-suited) to being used as formative assessment activities?

Assessment activity	L/R?	What are the pupils doing?	Issues in relation to formative assessment
e.g. A text comprising a series of single sentences (each numbered) describing hobbies.	L or R	Matching the information in the text to pictures (with a designated letter).	Useful as a practice activity but less effective as a formative assessment activity, because it is difficult to identify which aspect of the task may have been easy/less easy for the pupil.
e.g. A text focusing on a number of teenagers in the target country describing hobbies, including other related details (frequency, cost, the people with whom the hobby is carried out etc.).	L or R	Complete a table summarising the key information in relation to each of the speakers/writer.	Opportunity to assess the outcomes and give pupils feedback based on their strengths and the things they need to develop in terms of their listening/reading skills. Opportunity to discuss strategies for effective listening/reading with individuals or the whole class. Opportunity to give group feedback in relation to common errors/misconceptions. Opportunities for peer and/or self-assessment.
etc. ……..			

THE ROLE OF CORRECTIVE FEEDBACK

The way in which corrective feedback (CF) is given to the learners in relation to the errors they make is not a straightforward process and the approaches taken by any teacher may reflect a complex set of understandings as to the way in which language is acquired. Indeed, there has been significant debate over a number of years, drawing on research that is informed by differing theoretical positions in relation to the effective use of CF. Ellis (2009, p. 14) summarises the nature of these controversies and concludes with a set of useful suggestions as to how CF might be used effectively in the classroom:

1   Teachers should ascertain their students' attitudes towards CF, apprise them of the value of CF, and negotiate agreed goals for CF with them. The goals are likely to vary according to the social and situational context.

2   CF (both oral and written) works and so teachers should not be afraid to correct students' errors. This is true for both accuracy and fluency work, so CF has a place in both.

3   Focused CF is potentially more effective than unfocused CF, so teachers should identify specific linguistic targets for correction in different lessons. This will occur naturally in accuracy work based on a structure-of-the-day approach but can also be usefully applied in fluency work.

4   Teachers should ensure that learners know they are being corrected (i.e., they should not attempt to hide the corrective force of their CF moves from the learners). Whereas it will generally be clear to learners that they are being corrected in the case of written CF, it may not always be clear in the case of oral CF.

5   Teachers need to be able to implement a variety of oral and written CF strategies and to adapt the specific strategies they use to the particular learner they are correcting. One way of doing this is to start with a relatively implicit form of correction (e.g., simply indicating that there is an error) and, if the learner is unable to self-correct, to move to a more explicit form (e.g., a direct correction). This requires that teachers be responsive to the 'feedback' they get from learners on their own CF.

6   Oral CF can be both immediate and delayed. Teachers need to experiment with the timing of the CF. Written CF is almost invariably delayed.

7   Teachers need to create space following the corrective move for learners to uptake the correction. However, whether the correction is or is not appropriated should be left to the learner (i.e., the teacher should not require the learner to produce the correct form). In the case of written CF, learners need the opportunity to attend to the corrections and revise their writing.

8   Teachers should be prepared to vary who, when, and how they correct in accordance with the cognitive and affective needs of the individual learner. In effect this means they do not need to follow a consistent set of procedures for all students.

9   Teachers should be prepared to correct a specific error on several occasions to enable the learner to achieve full self-regulation.

10 Teachers should monitor the extent to which corrective feedback causes anxiety in learners and should adapt the strategies they use to ensure that anxiety facilitates rather than debilitates.

Task 4.7

Giving corrective feedback

Audio-record two or three lessons in which you know that there are likely to be examples of oral interaction between you and the pupils, or where you know that there will be speaking activities that will involve you listening to the pupils and responding.

Listen to the recordings at a later stage and transcribe some of the examples of where you gave any sort of corrective feedback to the pupils.

Analyse these records of the interactions and think about them in relation to the guidelines suggested by Ellis (2009).

Is there anything that you would change, were you to be doing a similar exercise, in order to make the corrective feedback that you gave more effective?

It might also be useful to carry out a similar exercise with a colleague/colleagues and to share a discussion based on the data that you each collect.

CONCLUSION

The conscious use of formative assessment in the classroom can be an invaluable tool to help develop the pupils' foreign language skills. It is, however, an approach that needs to be integrated fully into the language learning process and will only be effective if there is an underlying understanding of the principles behind it and a commitment to putting these principles into practice in the classroom. Research has shown that such an approach leads to improvements in levels of attainment (Black and Wiliam, 1998) and it is also not difficult to see the positive effect that it can have on levels of pupil motivation. If we are to raise the levels of achievement of the pupils we teach then we should be keen to develop our own practice in this area and provide pupils with overwhelmingly positive experiences of the assessment process.

REFERENCES

Assessment Reform Group (2002) *Assessment for Learning: 10 Principles.* Available at http://www.assessment-reform-group.org.uk

Black, P. and Jones, J. (2006) 'Formulative assessment and the learning and teaching of MFL: sharing the language learning road map with the learners'. *The Language Learning Journal*, 34(1), 4–9.

Black, P. and Wiliam, D. (1998) *Inside the Black Box: Raising Standards Through Classroom Assessment.* London: King's College.

Department for Education (2011) *Teachers' Standards.* Available at http://www.education.gov.uk/publications

Ellis, R. (2009) 'Corrective feedback and teacher development'. *L2 Journal*, 1(1), 3–18. Available at http://escholarship.org/uc/item/2504d6w3

Pachler, N., Evans, M., Redondo, A. and Fisher, L. (2014) *Learning to Teach Foreign Languages in the Secondary School.* 4th edition. London: Routledge.

Wiliam, D. (2011) 'What is assessment for learning?' *Studies in Educational Evaluation*, 37(1), 3–14.

Chapter 5   Developing listening skills in a foreign language

GARY N. CHAMBERS

BY THE END OF THIS CHAPTER YOU SHOULD:

- have a clear understanding of the complexity of listening;
- have gained some insight into the factors which may make listening difficult for some pupils;
- have an understanding of how to exploit a listening text as a 'learning experience' rather than a 'test';
- have acquired some ideas for listening tasks which might put the pupils more in control of their own listening.

WHAT IS IT AND WHY BOTHER WITH IT?

What is it?

As a student, I spent my summers working as a labourer on a building site. Each year one of my naïve fellow students was invariably sent by one of the tradesmen to the supplies hut for 'a long stand'. The worker in charge of supplies, familiar with the joke, told the unsuspecting student to wait. Of course the student was made to wait and wait and wait – a long stand.

What lessons can be learned from this?

- Speaker and listener have to be operating within the same context for understanding to be facilitated. Could the student have known that the tradesman was playing a joke? Did the student know what a 'long stand' was, what it looked like or why it was needed?
- The listener should take advantage of any paralinguistic cues which may be on offer. Was the tradesman smirking as he gave the instruction? Was there anything about his body language or tone of voice which suggested that something was not quite right?

Listening is neither a simple nor a passive activity. The listener has to bring much to the process:

- knowledge of the topic of the listening text;
- knowledge of the language;
- the ability to recognise and discriminate between individual sounds;

- the ability to pick out the main points from the redundant material;
- the ability to fill in gaps left by the speaker.

Listening is both a complex and an active activity (Vandergrift, 2008).

Why bother with it?

Listening is integral to the language learning process. Listening rarely takes place in isolation from other skills and usually happens in tandem with them, most commonly speaking. It is a rich source of material for consolidating known language and giving access to unknown language which can (and often should) be recycled. It has a contribution to make to pupils' listening skills in general, not just the foreign language (FL). This is reflected in the skills identified in documents such as *The Languages Ladder* (Department for Children, Schools and Family, 2007) and *The Common European Framework of Reference for Languages: Learning, Teaching, Assessment* (Council of Europe, 2011). Such skills include: listening for gist and detail; listening for subtleties; listening for inferences; recognising rhetorical devices. Listening material can be found in an interesting and varied range of sources (TV, film, DVD, radio, theatre, internet, conversation), contributing to learning in general, interests and hobbies, cultural insights and entertainment.

WHAT MAKES IT DIFFICULT?

In survey after survey pupils put listening activities at the bottom or next to the bottom (after writing) of their list of least enjoyed FL activities (see Chambers, 1993 and 1998). Pupils generally complain that the pace of the target language (TL) speech is too fast and so the meaning is inaccessible and the related tasks are too difficult. In certain cases, these pupil perceptions may be accurate. It may also be the case, however, that the pupils are being prepared insufficiently for meeting the challenge of the listening activity.

In a large furniture store, I overheard a customer asking her partner: 'Have you seen those delicious suites?' Imagine that this had been recorded for use in a language learning class. Given that in most schools the recording would be on CD, the pupils would not have access to the paralinguistic cues which would help them understand the context of the customer's question. They would also need to have quite sophisticated knowledge of language to distinguish between 'suites' and 'sweets' and to appreciate the interestingly ambiguous use of 'delicious'. Although some schools provide pupils with laptops to facilitate learner autonomy, in most cases the teacher, rather than the pupils, would have control of the replay facility and would determine how much was heard at one go and how often the whole listening text was heard. This may help illustrate some of the problems listeners face.

Listening is challenging. Listeners need to bring a range of scaffolding to the experience:

- knowledge of the context;
- knowledge of the topic;
- knowledge of language.

If pupils are to enjoy listening activities, their knowledge of the above areas needs to be triggered as part of the preparation for the activity. To fail to do so, leads to pupils tackling the activity 'cold', without the knowledge that they would normally have in an authentic listening context. When they go to the bakery in their home town, for example, they are aware of the sort of language they are going to hear and use. When they go to the bakery in a French town, they will probably rehearse the language they are going to use on the way to the bakery and predict the sort of language they are going to hear; visual clues (facial expression; body language; pointing) will also be available to support understanding and communication.

How can we move more towards providing pupils with the strategies and scaffolding they need to succeed in and enjoy listening activities?

LISTENING AS A TEST *VERSUS* LISTENING AS A LEARNING EXPERIENCE

The teacher hands out the worksheet; s/he tells the pupils to be quiet, to listen to the recording (to be played twice) and to tick the boxes as appropriate; the teacher goes through the answers with the pupils. This is a very crude version of a listening *test*. It could be made less crude. Instructions could be given in the TL. The teacher might go through the worksheet to ensure understanding. The task might be something more imaginative than ticking boxes. Nevertheless, it is a *test*. Tests do have their place. After all, pupils will have to engage in listening tests at GCSE and Advanced levels. If, however, pupils are to become more skilled listeners, *tests* should not be the norm. *Tests* should be transformed into *learning experiences* (see White, 2001).

What follows are a number of principles which underpin listening as a *learning experience*. (See also Rost, 2002.) Some of these might usefully be shared with pupils, to enhance their understanding of the listening process and the strategies (Vandergrift, 2008) which might be employed:

- Pupils are more likely to be receptive to listening texts and tasks, if their purpose is made clear and the importance of the content is understood. Bone (1998) reports that people often listen at only 25% of their potential and ignore, forget, distort or misunderstand the other 75%. Concentration rises above 25% if they think that what they are hearing is important and/or they are interested in it, but it never reaches 100%.
- We do not have to understand every word in order to understand the essence of the text. Depending on our perception of what we need to understand (consider the difference between listening to instructions on how to drive a car and listening to the evening news), we listen as extensively as possible and intensively as necessary.
- Listening is not a passive but an active process.
- Strategies for understanding include: concentrating on what is understood; distinguishing between the important and the unimportant; exploitation of what is already known about the topic.
- A relaxed atmosphere opens up all the senses (see Good and Brophy, 1994; Solmecke, 1992).
- The level of difficulty is determined not by the text but by the task.
- Hypothesis testing is part of learning to listen (and of learning a language). It is OK to get something wrong. We learn from our mistakes.

LISTENING AS A LEARNING EXPERIENCE – A CONCRETE EXAMPLE

This particular text was chosen because a) it is a poem, a style different from the usual dialogue, DVD or radio excerpt; b) the topic is included in all GCSE specifications and is also likely to come up in authentic conversations with native speakers; c) it lends itself to being learnt by heart, not least because the rhythm makes the reciting fun.

Meine Woche

Am Montag fahre ich Fahrrad.	*On Monday I ride my bike.*
Am Dienstag sehe ich fern.	*On Tuesday I watch TV.*
Am Mittwoch spiele ich Fußball.	*On Wednesday I play football.*
Das mache ich sehr, sehr gern.	*I like that very much.*
Am Donnerstag, da schwimmen wir.	*On Thursday we go swimming.*
Am Freitag spiele ich Klavier.	*On Friday I play piano.*
Am Samstag kommt Frau Stange.	*On Saturday Frau Stange comes.*
Am Sonntag schlafe ich lange.	*On Sunday I have a lie in.*
Und schon höre ich die Mama:	*And already I can hear my mum:*
"Komm Peter! Steh auf! Schule!"	*"Come on Peter. Get up. Time for school!"*
Ja, dann ist der Montag da.	*Yes, it's Monday.*

(Source: Seeger, H. (1985) *Wer? Wie? Was?* Schülerbuch Stufe 1. Gilde, p.56)

Pre-listening phase

As the term suggests, the pre-listening phase precedes the first playing of the recording. Pre-listening activities serve a number of purposes:

- to put the text into context;
- to stimulate pupils' knowledge of the topic;
- to stimulate the pupils' knowledge of language associated with the topic;
- to arouse expectations of what the text might contain;
- to arouse curiosity.

Such activities might include:

- discussion of a picture;
- a short piece of reading;
- brain-storming;
- setting a scene and asking the pupils to predict what happens next.

(For further examples see Dahlhaus, 1994; Underwood, 1989.)

Task 5.1

Pre-listening activities

Looking at the poem 'Meine Woche', think of possible pre-listening activities. Consider the following questions:

- How are you going to access how much vocabulary the pupils already know about free-time activities?
- How are you going to make them curious about the poem they are going to read a little later in the lesson?
- How are you going to introduce key words contained in the poem, which will help the pupils understand the poem?

Suggestions:

- Put a diary in a bag; invite a pupil to come to the front of the class; show her/ him the contents; the rest of the class then has to establish what is in the bag by asking questions which may only be answered by 'yes' or 'no'. Depending on the level of ability of the class, this might be done in the TL. This could then lead to revision of days, months, possible diary entries.
- Thought-shower/Brainstorming/Spidergram – on the topic of leisure-time activities.
- Provide the pupils with six or seven key words which come up in the poem (e.g. *Montag/Mittwoch/Samstag/Frau Stange/Klavier/Fußball/Schule*) and ask them to write a short story including these words.

For other pre-listening ideas, see Dahlhaus (1994).

While-listening phase

In this phase the text is played to the pupils for the first time. It has two parts.

Part 1 includes activities to access pupils' global understanding of the text, its broad content and/or general message. It also gives pupils the opportunity to tune into the speed at which people speak, their mood, accent and any background noises. Activities, therefore, usually take the form of broad questions, such as:

- How many people are speaking?
- Where are they?
- Are they happy/sad/angry?

See also Dahlhaus (1994) and http:www.zut.org.uk. This website provides a host of activities (French, German, Spanish and Welsh) which could easily be adapted to provide tasks which access pupils' global understanding.

Again, depending on the pupils' level of language, this phase may be conducted in the TL. They should be made aware that they will hear the tape as often as they need to.

Task 5.2

Global understanding

Thinking about the poem above, what might you use as appropriate while-listening activities to access *global understanding*?

Consider the following questions:

- What activities would give the pupils a reason to listen to the text without forcing them to listen to detailed information or language with which they might not be familiar?
- Could a kinaesthetic approach be adopted?

Suggestions:

- Put your hand up when you hear a day of the week.
- Stand up when you hear someone's name.
- How many of the activities on the spidergram, which we developed on the board, do you hear on the tape?

The answers provided by the pupils can of course be developed further (in the TL) to revise more known material, e.g. what's the second/fifth/sixth day of the week? Can we think of six other German names? Can we remember five other activities without looking at the spidergram?

Now that the pupils are tuned into the pace, context and language of the tape, they are ready for while-listening Part 2, which accesses their detailed understanding of the text.

Such activities might include:

- questions and answers in English/German;
- true/false;
- multiple choice;
- listen and draw;
- listen and follow the instructions;
- listen and identify the face/person/animal which matches the description;
- listen and fill in the gap in the text.

Again, pupils should be made aware that they will hear the tape as often as they need to. This gives them a number of opportunities to modify any initial conclusions they may have drawn to support the transition from global to detailed understanding.

Task 5.3

Detailed understanding

Looking at the poem, what sort of activities might be appropriate in this phase for accessing **detailed understanding**?
Consider the following:

- What language do you want the pupils to remember and recycle (see post-listening phase below)?
- What activities would allow you to stay in the TL but still access pupils' comprehension of the text (rather than facilitate regurgitation of sections of the text)?

Can you think of an activity which might be just a little bit different?

Suggestions:

- Listen and put the jumbled text/jumbled pictures in the appropriate order.
- Correct the factual inaccuracies.
- Fill in the missing activities in the appropriate gaps in the transcript/chart.
- Answer the questions in German.
- Mime the activities as you hear them.

You may wish to try out other while-listening activities at the following websites:
http://www.zut.org.uk
http://www.bbc.co.uk/schools/gcsebitesize

Post-listening phase

In the course of the pre- and while-listening activities, pupils will have consolidated known vocabulary and perhaps grammatical structures (e.g. verb inversion) and accessed some new language. The post-listening phase should be exploited to recycle this. How might this be done in the case of this poem?

Task 5.4

Multi-skill exploitation

Consider the following:

- How can the listening text stimulate a multi-skill learning experience, that is, one which includes one or more of listening, speaking, writing and reading?
- Is there an opportunity here for pair and group work?
- Can you provide pupils, in this phase, with a real or plausible reason to speak/write/read?

Suggestions:

- Pupils write their own poem, based on the structure of *Meine Woche*.
- With their partner, they write a dialogue based on what they do each day.
- They write a letter or email message to their class-link in Germany or to another set in their year group (a 'real' readership) about what they do in their spare time.

Putting the pupils in control

Nothing is so good that it cannot be improved. White (2001) identifies some problems with the above procedure:

- Classroom listening very often puts the students in the position of 'passive overhearers' – artificiality of listening to a recording; the listener cannot stop, interrogate or interact; the teacher is in control.
- Not much time is spent actually listening to the recording – quite a lot on discussing the answers and doing transfer activities.
- Not much time is spent analysing what went wrong – how do students mishear or fail to hear? – we focus on the product of listening rather than the process.

White (2001) suggests that approaches should be adopted which allow pupils to:

- reflect on their problems in understanding and on strategies they could use to overcome problems. This can only be taught effectively by interrupting the listening process and getting students to reflect on what they have just been doing;
- become active participants in the listening process rather than 'passive overhearers';
- control the equipment;

- give the instructions;
- choose what they listen to;
- design the listening tasks; and
- make their own listening materials.

Task 5.5

Active listening

How can some of the above be addressed in practical terms?

Suggestions:

- Pupils record an interview with their exchange class to be published in the departmental magazine or on the virtual learning environment (VLE).
- Pupils make a radio play in groups – others have to judge which is best.
- Listening task as part of carousel of activities.
- Exploitation of software and/or internet as a source of listening texts.
- Listening homework – pupils use CD/DVD/internet.
- Pupils provide exercises to go with texts.
- Provide a box of differentiated listening materials, following the model of *Bibliobus* (Mary Glasgow Publications, 1983) and *Lesekiste* (Mary Glasgow Publications, 1986) for pupils to access themselves in the course of an autonomous listening session. (Working on listening texts autonomously, however, is not problem-free; see Graham, 2007.) Pupils could contribute to this, for example, by providing listening materials they may have come across themselves; developing exploitation tasks to accompany the texts; writing critiques of the texts/tasks. Morgan and Neil (2001) provide some useful ideas involving the Foreign language Assistant (FLA) who could record and provide the following:
  - ○ 'talking books';
  - ○ tongue-twisters and nursery rhymes;
  - ○ listening discrimination exercises;
  - ○ 'attitude' tapes where things are said demonstrating different emotions;
  - ○ pop songs and accompanying transcriptions.

A good starting point for giving pupils more control of their listening might be:

- http://www.ashcombe.surrey.sch.uk/Curriculum/modlang/index_teaching. htm
  This site provides more than 80 mini videos in French, German, Spanish and Italian with interactive self-marking quizzes. Students have the facility to start, stop and pause the videos as they feel the need and can also access hints for support.
- http://www.languageguide.org/ contains a range of listening material (with transcripts) on a variety of topics in a number of languages. This site allows pupils to work on tasks related to their own textbook.
- http://www.glogster.com/ allows pupils to access videos and audio recordings, amongst a range of other resources.

- http://www.euronews.net provides authentic video/audio clips with summaries and transcripts.
- http://ww.tes.co.uk provides all manner of topic-related listening (including high quality video clips) and other resources, including quizzes and games.

CONCLUSION

Listening plays an integral role in the language learning process. Pupils do not generally regard listening tasks as motivating or enjoyable. Even the 'success stories', those who continue with language beyond GCSE, find listening difficult and anxiety-inducing (Graham, 2006). Something has to be done to change this state of affairs. I maintain that a *learning experience* approach, even with its faults, is more likely to reach the parts of pupils' motivation that the *test* cannot reach. Combine this with putting the pupils more in control, and their perceptions of listening and their listening skills could change for the better.

REFERENCES

Bone, D. (1988) *A Practical Guide to Effective Listening.* London: Kogan Page.

Chambers, G. (1998) 'Pupils' perceptions of the foreign language learning experience'. *Language Teaching Research,* 2(3), 231–259.

Chambers, G. (1993) 'Taking the de- out of demotivation'. *Language Learning Journal,* 7(1), 1–6.

Council of Europe (2011) *Common European Framework of Reference for Languages: Learning, Teaching, Assessment.* Available at http://www.coe.int/t/DG4/Portfolio/?L=E&M=/documents_intro/Data_bank_descriptors.html

Dahlhaus, B. (1994) *Fertigkeit Hören.* Berlin/München: Langenscheidt.

Department for Children, Schools and Family (2007) *The Languages Ladder.* London: DCSF.

Good, T. and Brophy, J. (1994) *Looking in Classrooms.* New York: HarperCollins.

Graham, S. (2006) 'Listening comprehension: the learners' perspective'. *System,* 34(2), 165–182.

Graham, S. (2007) 'Learner strategies and self-efficacy: making the connection'. *Language Learning Journal,* 35(1), 81–93.

Levine, G. (2003) 'Student and instructor beliefs and attitudes about target language use, first language use, and anxiety: report of a questionnaire study'. *The Modern Language Journal,* 87(3), 343–364.

Mary Glasgow Publications (1983) *Bibliobus.* Southam: MGP.

Mary Glasgow Publications (1986) *Lesekiste.* Southam: MGP.

Morgan, C. and Neil, P. (2001) *Teaching Modern Foreign Languages.* London: Kogan Page.

Rost, M. (2002) *Teaching and Researching: Listening.* Harlow: Pearson Education.

Solmecke, G. (1992) 'Ohne Hören kein Sprechen'. *Fremsprache Deutsch* 7, 4–11.

Underwood, M. (1989) *Teaching Listening.* Longman: London.

Vandergrift, L. (2008) 'Learning strategies for listening comprehension'. In Hurd, S. and Lewis, T. (eds) *Language Learning Strategies in Independent Settings.* Clevedon: Multilingual Matters, pp. 84–102.

White, G. (2001) *Listening.* Oxford: Oxford University Press.

Chapter 6   Developing speaking skills in a foreign language

SUZANNE GRAHAM

BY THE END OF THIS CHAPTER YOU SHOULD:

- have gained insights into common problems associated with speaking in the foreign language (FL);
- have acquired some ideas for overcoming these problems;
- have a clear understanding of what makes a successful speaking activity;
- have learnt how to incorporate such activities into the framework of a lesson.

THE CHALLENGE OF ORAL WORK

Research into pupils' perceptions of speaking in the FL presents us with something of a paradox. Anecdotal and research evidence (e.g. Busse & Williams, 2010) suggests that many learners feel that being able to communicate orally is an important goal in FL learning. It is something that many learners see as enjoyable (Chambers, 1999). Yet it is also the skill in which learners at the end of Key Stage 4 feel they have had the least success (Graham, 2002), and which seems to cause them anxiety (Gallagher-Brett, 2007). Over a number of years, in its summary reports on FL teaching in England, OFSTED has repeatedly commented on pupils' lack of confidence in speaking at length or with fluency, and their lack of ability to speak spontaneously or to say what they want to say and the negative impact that has on pupil motivation for FL, with the 2008 and 2011 reports expressing these concerns perhaps most strongly.

Task 6.1

Expectations

What is expected of learners nationally in terms of speaking skills? Consult the National Curriculum Orders and a GCSE specification. Outline what the Programme of Study says about the types of speaking skills pupils are expected to develop and how progression in speaking is characterised (for Key Stage 3) and in GCSE grades (for Key Stage 4). At what level are learners expected to be able to speak with some spontaneity?

Factors impacting on speaking

Think back to classes you have observed in Key Stages 3 and 4. Do you agree with the judgement of OFSTED (2011) that pupils lack confidence in speaking at length with fluency, or independently/spontaneously? If so, what factors might contribute to pupils' under-developed speaking skills?

Reasons you might suggest for pupils' under-developed speaking skills are:

- learners are given speaking tasks that fail to motivate them to speak;
- speaking tasks are set that offer learners few opportunities to use the language independently or spontaneously;
- learners lack the 'tools' to overcome gaps in their vocabulary to say what they want to say and to keep the conversation going;
- anxiety on the part of learners, which makes them reluctant to take risks in using the language, perhaps for fear of making a mistake or losing face in front of peers, especially if there is a focus on accuracy in the classroom;
- a lack of focus on meaningful interaction within whole-class oral work.

Possible solutions

Looking at the above list, one factor seems to stand out as an area that we need to focus on if we are to be successful in developing learners' speaking skills – the nature of the speaking tasks that we set them, and the quality of the interaction in which we ask learners to engage. For pupils to speak in the FL, they have to *want* to speak or be motivated to do so. This seems an obvious statement, but one that unfortunately is not always put into practice.

Task 6.3

Motivating pupils to speak

Think back to a speaking activity you have observed or in which you have participated yourself, where learners seemed motivated to speak. Can you identify any factors that might have contributed to making the speaking activity motivating?

EFFECTIVE SPEAKING TASKS

Ur (1996) gives a comprehensive list of factors that are common to successful speaking activities, including: learners talk a lot; participation is evenly distributed; motivation is high; meaningful information is being communicated. It could be argued that the first two of these factors are in turn influenced by the extent to which learners feel comfortable about speaking, uninhibited by any feelings of anxiety.

Task 6.4

Observing speaking activities

Arrange to observe a class and focus on the following areas:

- In whole-class speaking activities (for example, question and answer), roughly what proportion of the class gets to speak? Do some pupils never or rarely speak in such situations? Why not, do you think?
- What kind of language are pupils producing in whole-class situations? Single words, sentences?
- Where pupils produce more extended answers, what kinds of questions have prompted these responses?
- How are errors in whole-class oral work dealt with by the teacher?
- When learners are engaged in pair or group speaking activities, do they make more or fewer errors than in whole-class speaking situations?
- Does the teacher do anything to correct any errors made in pair or group activities?

High participation, low anxiety

From your observations you have probably concluded that most learners feel less comfortable when speaking in a whole-class situation than when discussing in a pair or small group. Even adults find the second situation the least anxiety-inducing and the most conducive to the free expressions of opinions.

As well as lowering pupil anxiety, speaking activities that involve pair or small group work have another big advantage over whole-class work – they increase the amount of time that each learner spends speaking the TL. Choral repetition does allow lots of learners to speak at once, but rarely involves learners using the language in anything but an imitative and rather narrow way. In question and answer work, open-ended questions give pupils some opportunities to speak at greater length, and if they are genuine questions, requiring real information in the answer, then learners are more likely to be motivated to reply and to listen to the responses of other learners in the class. However, as Yang (2010) notes, such questions on their own do not guarantee that learners will give extended answers; teachers also need to give them sufficient time and encouragement to do so, by 'pushing' them to give more complex answers, that preferably include a verb. This is also argued by Macaro and Mutton (2002), who provide evidence that in whole-class oral interaction learners make very short, noun-based utterances unless the teacher consciously makes an effort to prompt them to give extended answers. Learners can be supported to extend their answers by prompt sheets that provide them with key phrases such as 'How do I say …', 'Can you repeat the question please?' They can also 'participate' even when the question is being posed to someone else, by being encouraged to answer the question in their head. Examples of prompt sheets for all these areas can be found in Macaro (2001) at http://pdcinmfl.com. Being engaged in the question and answer sequence is also more likely if some of the questions are asked by the learners, and responses are elicited from learners, rather than the teacher just taking responses from those with their hands up.

Another benefit of pair/group speaking activities is the impact that interaction and negotiation of meaning can have on language acquisition (Lightbown, 2003). Beginning teachers often worry that by working with peers, learners will somehow 'catch' each others' errors and that these errors need to be avoided/corrected as soon as possible. As Lightbown points out, there is very little research evidence to support this view. Indeed, if learners are to be encouraged to take risks with their speaking, the teacher needs to promote a classroom environment overall in which errors are regarded as part of the learning process and are corrected with sensitivity.

Purpose

Unfortunately, not all learners will value a speaking activity for its own sake, for the good that it might do their oral skills. Most will need an additional reason for completing a task, over and above the fact that you, the teacher, have asked them to complete it and told them that it would be useful for them to do so. In other words, the task needs to have a purpose. It also needs to have an end-goal, so that learners are encouraged to carry it through. Burch, Harris, Jones and Darcy (2001) use the helpful acronym 'PIFCO' to outline the key elements of an effective speaking task: Purpose, Information, Context, Feedback and Outcome. In terms of 'purpose', one of the most important attributes of a motivating speaking task is the incorporation of an 'information-gap element', the 'I' of this acronym. This means that real information is being exchanged by learners, that they are communicating in order to find out something that they need to know. Thus, in the following activity, learners have to ask questions and give responses in order to determine on which day and at which time they are both free to meet to go out. A separate sheet gives details of possible activities (e.g. films at the cinema, with showing times). At the end of the activity, each pair reports back on when they are meeting and what they are going to do when they meet.

Partenaire A		**Partenaire B**
LUNDI	Jean ici 20.00	LUNDI film télé 20.15
MARDI	Maison des Jeunes 19.00	MARDI
MERCREDI		MERCREDI Cinéma avec Alain 20.45
JEUDI	M. Bizet dîner chez nous	JEUDI football télé 19.30
VENDREDI		VENDREDI
SAMEDI	barbecue chez Paul 19.00	SAMEDI
DIMANCHE		DIMANCHE chez grands-parents

Reporting back (or feedback, from the teacher or one's pair work partner) is important for increasing the purpose of activities. Not only do speaking activities need to have a clear end-goal, but learners should also be aware at the start of the activity that the teacher will require some kind of feedback from them. This helps to ensure that they actually finish the task and gives it a sense of completeness. Follow-up can take many forms; for example, some pupils might be asked to perform certain aspects of the task to the rest of the class (with clear ground rules established about not laughing at or making fun of the 'performers'). Similarly, for other 'non-performing' learners to listen attentively, the feedback session needs to have a clearly stated purpose. This may be an evaluative one, with the teacher and/ or the rest of the class assessing how well learners have dealt with the speaking task. In addition, the class as a whole needs to be aware of the criteria by which the teacher is judging them – are they looking for fluency, accuracy? Other learners might also be asked to make suggestions about how the 'performers' could improve what they said, perhaps by paying attention to intonation in question forms (for French), thinking about correct word order (for German), etc. Or, and perhaps better, the class could listen out for specific information that they genuinely want to hear, perhaps the outcome of an information-gap activity.

Opportunities to say what one wants to say

Purpose also involves learners saying something personally relevant, and to express what they want to say, rather than just what the teacher wants them to say. So, for instance, Burch *et al.* (2001) give the example of a pair work activity on the topic of 'Places in the town'. In many coursebooks this would take the form of one learner asking the question (in the TL) 'What is there in your town?' and his/her partner simply responding with a list of places in the TL. A more meaningful version of this would be for the partner to identify the places in the town that are important to him/her, and to explain why. This sort of activity requires a restructuring and a manipulation of language that has initially been presented in a guided fashion. Phipps (1999) also gives a number of examples of speaking activities that incorporate a creative, 'personalising' element – including asking pupils to substitute their own words for items underlined in a dialogue, ranking items on a list (for example, items one might take to a desert island) and giving reasons for this ranking, adding a problem element to a role play (for example, in a restaurant role play, imagining that you are ordering for a friend who is a vegetarian). Of course, being able to add this creative element, and to manipulate known language, means that core structures needed to complete the speaking task have been thoroughly practised in a more controlled manner first of all (see also below).

Characteristics of a good speaking activity: a summary

- The activity is motivating: it has a clear purpose (beyond a 'language practice' purpose), and an end-goal or outcome with opportunities for meaningful feedback.
- Speaking opportunities are maximised, that is, the task cannot be completed by learners saying very little.
- The activity can be extended to allow pupils to speak more independently and to personalise the language used.

Task 6.5

Speaking and coursebooks

Look at a FL coursebook and focus on some of the speaking activities it includes. To what extent do they match the criteria for a good speaking activity given in this chapter? If they have any shortcomings, how might you improve them?

INCORPORATING PAIR/GROUP SPEAKING TASKS INTO LESSONS

It is important that before learners are set off on a pair or group speaking task, they have been introduced to and been given supported practice in much of the language that they will need to complete the activity. So, for example, if they are to conduct a survey to find out what pets classmates have at home, they need to be comfortable in both asking the relevant questions (*Hast du Haustiere? As-tu un animal à la maison?*) and giving a response to such questions.

Phipps (1999) gives detailed guidance in the stages that learners and teachers should go through in moving from whole-class oral work to pair work. The first is likely to involve some kind of modelling by the teacher of each piece of language, probably followed by whole-class repetition. Once the class as a group are comfortable with the language, the exchanges expected in the role play are then practised with the class, with different members of the group having the opportunity to take on each role. The teacher might begin by asking a question from the role play to individual pupils (teacher–pupil); then, individual pupils would be asked to pose the question to the teacher (pupil–teacher); next, some 'open pairs' practice might follow, in which a pupil in one part of the classroom would ask the question to another pupil on the other side of the room; finally, the teacher would ask two pupils to demonstrate the role play to the rest of the class, before setting all pupils off on the complete pair work activity with their partner. In this way, pupils are clear about what is required of them in the activity and are confident in the language that they need to use to complete it.

HELPING LEARNERS TO 'KEEP GOING' AND TO SAY THINGS THEY ARE UNSURE OF

We need to remember that once the language has been practised within such a structured framework as just outlined, learners should then be given the opportunity to go beyond this. This may, and arguably should, involve learners trying to say things they are unsure of. This is likely to help them to manipulate, recycle and make connections with the language they have already learned (Coyle, 2007). For this approach to be possible, certain conditions are important: the teacher needs to build in opportunities for more spontaneous, unplanned talk (perhaps having a five minute open-ended 'chat' session at the start of each lesson); the classroom atmosphere needs to be a supportive one, where mistakes are viewed as part of the learning process (Coyle, 2007; Crichton, 2009); and learners need to be taught explicitly communication strategies that enable them to make up for any gaps in their linguistic knowledge – i.e. taught how to cope when they do not know a certain word or phrase for what they want to say.

Macaro (2001) and Grenfell and Harris (1999) outline various ways in which teachers can help learners to develop communication strategies, including teaching them to use mime, gesture and intonation to convey meaning; also filler phrases in the TL (e.g. *alors* in French, *also* in German) to buy time while they endeavour to remember a word that they need in the conversation; the skill of paraphrase or circumlocution, where learners say what they want to say but use different words or structures; asking the person with whom they are speaking to repeat or speak more slowly. Gallagher-Brett (2001) provides evidence that such strategies can be taught successfully to Key Stage 3 learners. The value of these communication strategies is that they allow learners to stay in the conversation and thus increase their exposure to the TL, and the amount of time they spend using it. In addition, they help them to be involved in 'negotiation of meaning', which is held to be highly beneficial for effective language acquisition (see Gass, 2010 for an overview).

Gallagher-Brett (2001) also comments that the model of progression in speaking inherent in the National Curriculum acts as a barrier to teachers expecting more spontaneous speech from learners and being able to use communication strategies from an early stage in their language learning, as dealing with the unpredictable and giving unprepared responses are not expected of learners until rather late on.

CONCLUSION

In this chapter, I have tried to show that teachers can enable all learners to acquire the necessary skills to develop their speaking, by carefully selecting and structuring the types of speaking opportunities that they offer to learners, and by helping them to develop strategies that help them to say what they really want to say.

REFERENCES

Burch, J., Harris, V., Jones, B. and Darcy, J. (2001) *Something to Say: Promoting Spontaneous Classroom Talk.* London: CILT.

Busse, V. & Williams, M. (2010) 'Why German? Motivation of students studying German at English universities'. *Language Learning Journal,* 38(1), 67–85.

Chambers, G. (1999) *Motivating Language Learners.* Clevedon: Multilingual Matters.

Coyle, D. (2007) 'Strategic classrooms: learning communities which nurture the development of learner strategies'. *Language Learning Journal,* 35(1), 65–79.

Crichton, H. (2009) ''Value added' modern languages teaching in the classroom: an investigation into how teachers' use of classroom target language can aid pupils' communication skills'. *Language Learning Journal,* 37(1), 19–34.

Gallagher-Brett, A. (2001) 'Teaching communication strategies to beginners'. *Language Learning Journal,* 24(1), 53–61.

Gallagher-Brett, A. (2007) 'What do learners' beliefs about speaking reveal about their awareness of learning strategies?' *Language Learning Journal,* 35(1), 37–49.

Gass, S. (2010) 'The relationship between L2 input and L2 output', in E. Macaro (ed.) *Continuum Companion to Second Language Acquisition* (pp. 194–219). London: Continuum.

Graham, S. (2002) 'Experiences of learning French: a snapshot at years 11, 12 and 13'. *Language Learning Journal,* 25(1), 15–20.

Grenfell, M. and Harris, V. (1999) *Modern Languages and Learning Strategies in Theory and in Practice.* London: Routledge.

Lightbown, P. M. (2003) 'SLA research in the classroom/SLA research for the classroom'. *Language Learning Journal,* 28(1), 4–13.

Macaro, E. (2001) *Learning Strategies in Second and Foreign Language Classrooms.* London: Continuum.

Macaro, E. and Mutton, T. (2002) 'Developing language teachers through a co-researcher model'. *Language Learning Journal,* 25(1), 27–39.

OFSTED (2008) *The changing landscape of languages.* Available at: www.ofsted.gov.uk/resources/changing-landscape-of-languages

OFSTED (2011) *Modern Languages. Achievement and challenge 2007–2010.* Available at: http://www.ofsted.gov.uk/resources/modern-languages-achievement-and-challenge-2007-2010

Phipps, W. (1999) *Interaction in the Modern Languages Classroom.* London: CILT.

Ur, P. (1996) *A Course in Language Teaching Practice and Theory.* Cambridge: Cambridge University Press.

Yang, C. C. R. (2010) 'Teacher questions in second language classrooms: an investigation of three case studies'. *Asian EFL Journal,* 12(1),181–201. Also available at: http://repository.ied.edu.hk/dspace/handle/2260.2/10124

Chapter 7 Developing reading and writing skills in a foreign language

ELISABETH LAZARUS

BY THE END OF THIS CHAPTER YOU SHOULD:

- have an understanding of how reading and writing skills support the learner's wider foreign language (FL) development;
- have gained some insight into the factors which will help learners decode written texts;
- have an understanding of the role of scaffolds and models in the writing process;
- have acquired some examples of how we can engage pupils creatively in reading and writing tasks.

WHY FOCUS ON READING AND WRITING SKILLS?

Although many pupils and their teachers will perceive the development of listening and speaking skills as of paramount importance in the languages classroom, developing reading skills in a FL is a crucial skill, as when we read we see many different genres, styles and models of writing, and it also helps us expand our use of structures and vocabulary. Being able to write in the FL can support not only memory and retention, but also allows pupils the opportunity to communicate in a written form with young people in other countries and settings. The rise of texting and social media means that reading messages and writing comments on the lives of others have become ubiquitous in the world of teenagers. As teachers, we can use the power of technology together with more traditional methods to create a range of mixed learning opportunities in the classroom. This can also inject differences of energy and pace, independent learning versus paired or group tasks, quieter and noisier activities which can help overcome what can be overly long lessons, drawing out the best and most creative outcomes from pupils. Large scale reviews of the research into reading and writing have shown how complex the processes of reading and writing are (Erler and Finkbeiner, 2007; Manchon *et al.*, 2007), and research is not conclusive if literacy difficulties pupils experience in FLs classrooms are due to a lack of L1 literacy or if they have just not had enough exposure to and proficiency in an L2 (Koda, 2005).

HOW TO DEVELOP READING – CHOOSING TEXTS

Reading in the FL can be highly motivating as pupils can often access the gist of a text which is more difficult than texts they could produce themselves via a range of clues, including images and illustrations, cognates and text markers such as capital letters for nouns in German. Research has shown that there are 'complex interactions between text, setting, reader background, reading strategies, the L1 and L2, and reader decision making' (Erler and Finkbeiner, 2007, p. 188). This places great responsibility on the teacher to select texts using their knowledge of the particular class and pupils' experience of literacy at Primary or Secondary level to help set appropriate challenges. Using texts which might be at the right linguistic level in terms of tenses, structures and lexis that pupils are already familiar with, but which appear to be aimed at a much younger authentic target language (TL) audience, could have the opposite effect of that desired. The advent of easy access to internet sources and simple but sophisticated looking materials, being produced using even the most basic software, has enabled teachers and departments to generate and share creative semi-authentic texts. In the past, we have sometimes been too concerned about texts being 'authentic' and this could lead to materials being used which pupils in the TL communities would rarely read. Experience suggests that learners do not mind if a text has been adapted or written by the teacher especially for them, as long as there is a sense of surprise, humour or some sort of problem solving task involved. Providing tantalising written excerpts which demand critical thinking of pupils in order to puzzle these clues into some sort of coherent sequence of events or story can lead to surprising outcomes and very engaged pupils. Linking texts to films, books or characters, which are particularly popular and topical, can be a very successful strategy.

So texts can be cognitively challenging but tasks demanded of pupils in relation to these may be set at different levels of difficulty to allow for differentiation according to the needs of individuals or classes (Atkinson and Lazarus, 1997). ICT also enables differentiation by using different font size, length of text, images, headings and numerical and other factual details included. For more experienced learners the challenge of sourcing reading materials on the internet for themselves and their peers is an added bonus, as long as we ensure that pupils understand that a level of criticality towards sources of texts is required.

Task 7.1

Focus on differentiation

Chose a text from a textbook or the internet and consider how you could use this for both a Year 7 and a Year 9 class.

- Are there alterations you feel you would have to make to the text?
- What type of activities would you ask a Year 7 group to carry out and would these be very different from those for the Year 9 class?
- True/false; yes/no; multiple choice or open-ended questions may all be useful, but what other options are there?

READING STRATEGIES

Using textual clues enables pupils to read texts which are, or appear, more authentic and difficult than the pupils' actual productive level would indicate. In order for pupils to understand and be able to make meaning of such texts, teachers need to give sufficient time to develop key metacognitive skills, such as skimming and scanning, using visual clues for decoding and guessing and, of course, looking for cognates in relation to their first or other languages. It would be wrong to assume that pupils can transfer strategies automatically from L1 to L2 and hence some targeted practice and explicit teaching is required. Their awareness needs to be raised that a combination of different strategies might be the most successful approach. Pupils will be encouraged to use their understanding of the world, past experiences and common sense to help in this process. Simple exercises, such as underlining or highlighting known words first, allow pupils individually, in pairs or groups to move from the known to the unknown language, rather than to start with the daunting new language straight away. This is also to ensure that pupils do not feel that they can only read and understand a text if they are able to translate every word into their mother tongue or common language.

Working with a partner means that a pupil can bounce ideas off someone else, test hypotheses and help construct meaning and knowledge jointly (Mitchell and Myles, 1998) and such approaches are good language learning strategies for all learners. With time and experience pupils can become very adept at using a range of strategies, which could be termed both 'bottom-up' and 'top-down' (Macaro, 2003), where bottom-up refers to the comprehension of individual words or phrases and top-down focuses on using their wider understanding of the world in making sense of the text; strategies which can be modified and adapted, discussed and questioned jointly. If we want pupils to read, then they need to know how to use bilingual glossaries and dictionaries. Time invested in choosing dictionaries which can make life easier for pupils, by considering layout, font and colour, for example, and lesson time devoted to helping pupils decipher bilingual dictionaries really pays off in the longer term and encourages much more autonomous learning.

READING FOR PLEASURE

The amount of reading pupils carry out beyond texting and using social media in their first language may be quite limited. A class survey can easily establish what type of reading pupils do and enjoy and can give useful insights and pointers for the teacher. One way to encourage reading for pleasure (Swarbrick, 1998), rather than to respond to comprehension activities in the classroom, can be to schedule some reading sessions in the school library, purchase subscriptions to FL magazines or scour the language department for past reading schemes, which often feature many different types of text and some very good stories but which are/were written with pupils in mind who are learning a FL without immersion and for a limited time in classroom settings. Pupils at all levels and ages can really enjoy keeping reading logs or diaries where they make a record of what they have read, new words they have come across and their opinions of the reading materials, rather than answering questions on a text which can really kill off any pleasure.

Having somewhere more comfortable to sit and the opportunity to read aloud to a friend, without the teacher listening in, are often considered to be a real bonus by pupils, as are recordings of the stories by native speakers. Sound files can be easily generated for the use on devices such as MP3 players (for example using software such as Audacity available at http://audacity.sourceforge.net/). Electronic books created by pupils using multimedia (for example http://wordle.net) or PowerPoint with sound files and video clips embedded in the text have also been very popular, especially when these had a real audience of younger learners. These home-produced 'books' have the added bonus that they are easy to store on school servers and that they are written with an audience in mind. Experience suggests that pupils like to touch, feel and read real books and magazines as well as using electronic devices to access those kept on the school's intranet, for example.

Pupils tend to like being read to in the FL by the teacher, as long as the readings are supported by dramatic voices and illustrations. Reading aloud in the classroom can become a real ordeal for self-conscious teenagers, but we should not underestimate how important it is to link the sound of words or letter strings to spellings if we want to combat the interference from the L1 (Macaro, 2003). One way to overcome this is for the teacher to start reading the text and to stop at random places for pupils to provide the next word or phrase as given in the text, or to offer an alternative which they prefer. Younger pupils are familiar with the role phonics can play in learning to read English; we should not overlook the importance of phonology in relation to L2.

Task 7.2

Monitoring reading

'Reading for pleasure' could imply enjoying a story or a text for the sake of the story without having 'to do' anything in response. How could you monitor the reading in the classroom or at home without this appearing as comprehension questions?

READING FOR GRAMMATICAL AWARENESS

Seeing models of well written texts allows teachers to draw their pupils' attention to grammatical or orthographical features that they want to teach or revise. Encouraging comparisons between texts can add sophistication and creativity to their own writing.

Sequencing chunks of text or paragraphs into a coherent order can help pupils see the application of time phrases and tenses. Texts can highlight how adjectives and adverbs can be used to instil particular moods or messages. Pupils can find deciphering abbreviated SMS text messages in the FL, used as starter activities for example, really enjoyable even when it meant converting abbreviations into full and grammatically accurate text.

In cases where short stories or novels have been turned into videos or films, an easy strategy to encourage older pupils to read texts intensively is to give half the class an extract from the text to read silently facing the opposite direction of the rest of the class who are watching the corresponding sequence on screen without sound. Pairs or groups then get together to compare the visual interpretation with the text. Naturally, in order to generate discussion and disagreement the text would include some subtle (or not so subtle) differences which pupils should notice. Watching film clips without sound and reading texts silently can have a remarkable effect on the classroom, leading to intense watching/reading and much greater concentration, and splitting the class into watching and reading, rather than everyone doing the same task, can work successfully.

One approach to the transition from reading to writing, which tends to work particularly with intermediate learners, is to do a 'jigsaw reading task', where individuals are given different texts to read about the same theme or topic and are then in groups asked to evaluate which text they prefer and why, which text appears most factual or most complex, for example. Outcomes can be a new piece of jointly created writing.

Task 7.3

Contrasting text with film clip

Choose a clip 2–4 minutes long from a video or from YouTube that you think will appeal to one of your classes and which is appropriate in content. Transcribe what you see into a text of one to two paragraphs including some clear differences from the video or ask your FLA to do this for you. Let half the class watch the clip twice without sound whilst the others have their backs to the screen, and read and underline key words. Pairs can then draw up a 'spot the difference' list. The whole class can view the clip one final time without sound and a joint consensus could be reached. Depending on the clip you choose, the TL culture could be a major feature of the comparison.

STRATEGIES TO DEVELOP WRITING

Being able to express oneself in writing can have real benefits and is essential for our examination system. Writing in the FL tends to start by noting down vocabulary and pertinent information linked to listening or reading tasks, matching words with symbols or drawings. Soon we find pupils completing forms and diagrams, writing shopping lists, composing post cards and letters and moving on to longer texts, summaries, reviews and essays.

In order for pupils to become confident writers they require models and scaffolds, practice and feedback on a regular basis. Watching primary level teachers encourage pupils' writing in their L1 can be a real eye opener and working closely with your English secondary colleagues can be equally beneficial. As teachers we need to be sensitive to the fact that many of our pupils are very good writers in their L1 but can benefit from a more step-by-step approach to gain confidence, accuracy and creativity in the FL. This could include 'think aloud' approaches where teachers talk through their writing strategies in front of the class. From an early stage pairs or groups of pupils benefit from improving the bare 'skeletons' of texts, as this can lead to very intensive scrutiny of the text and the language they already know. Macaro's own research (2003) and his review of the wider literature have shown that descriptive tasks are the easiest for L2 pupils to write, followed by narrative and discursive tasks. His research found evidence that responding to prose prompts (such as writing a response to a letter or email) 'produced writing samples with the best overall quality, the greatest fluency and the greatest syntactic complexity and highest accuracy' (Macaro, 2003, p. 224). However, too much exposure to descriptive writing only is not recommended and a balance needs to be struck across writing tasks and styles, although teachers need to be aware that descriptive tasks 'require a greater focus on nouns and adjectives whereas narration tasks require a high verb density. Discursive tasks involve high levels of idiomatic, phrasal verb knowledge plus the ability to generate complex sentences' (Macaro, 2003, p. 225).

TECHNOLOGY, CREATIVITY AND WRITING

Technology can be an excellent tool for supporting writing because editing and redrafting texts, after self-reflection, feedback from a peer or a teacher, is now so easy. Experimenting with language and making mistakes is much less daunting. Pupils can be introduced to mind maps helping them connect ideas and chunks of language they already know. However, they also need to understand the pitfalls of translation tools and websites.

Word processing can also have other benefits in the scaffolding of writing. Together with a colleague, I started to develop electronic writing frames with drop down menus, which gave pupils a range of synonyms, structures, conjugated verbs etc. which they could choose from before they attempted their own versions of writing (Gall *et al.*, 2008). We initially used the writing frames with very reluctant writers, and found that this was a great scaffold to help them practise different types of writing and to significantly improve length, content and written accuracy. Some writing frames look like flow diagrams while the intention of others is to act as a guide to the drafting stage. The role of the teacher and/or the peer is to ask questions when the writing frames are used. Why did the pupils choose the particular verb, this adjective over that, decide to use a different word order? This encourages critical thinking, the use of glossaries and dictionaries and drawing on peers, which may make pupils more autonomous in the busy language classroom.

You will often hear and see beginners and intermediate learners of the FL do their initial preparation and drafting in their L1; this is not surprising and should not cause us concern, but will lead to teachers having to mediate the tension between the sophistication which pupils would like to employ and their current knowledge of the FL. Research has found that the use of L1 in planning can be very beneficial and that pupils will employ many strategies, such as retrieving previously learnt phrases, recombining and restructuring language, as well as translation, to generating new text.

In recent years, technology has enabled pupils to be part of a writing community using a Wiki (see http://www.wikispaces.com/) to create a joint piece of writing where the text emerges jointly and can be edited using their combined understanding and knowledge. Teachers are encouraging pupils to post messages and thoughts on password protected Blogs (see htttp://edublogs.org) and to write scripts for their chosen Avatars, which Vokis (http://www.voki.com) now enable, injecting a new lease of life into tired topics. 'Running dictations' which have been very popular in the past, as they use reading, memorisation, careful spelling in order for groups of pupils to reconstruct texts posted on classroom walls, can now be carried out via QR codes, in classrooms where pupils are allowed to use smart devices (see http://qrcode.kaywa.com).

Visual stimuli, such as striking photos or post cards of paintings, are simple tools which can help stir creativity and encourage reluctant writers to have a go. A very successful sequence of lessons (Year 8) can be started by giving pupils striking photographs of people from all over the world and the country where these were taken. In pairs pupils research food and drink in the country or region and, with the help of a writing frame, write a simple text in German which also includes comparatives with food in England. They can be encouraged to comment on dietary habits due to drought, poverty or religion, for example. Paper plates can be decorated to represent the food and pairs present their findings to the rest of the class. Texts and plates can become a very colourful and informative display. This is a simple way of making writing more meaningful and culturally more relevant, as engaging pupils through a 'creative twist' is one way of making them more willing to write. For writing frames, see also Chapter 10 in Pachler, Evans, Redondo and Fisher, 2014.

Reading and writing can be seen as closely linked and mutually supporting.

Task 7.4

Scaffolding writing

Decide on the written outcome you are hoping your pupils are going to achieve, work backwards to their current starting point. What new language are you going to have to introduce? What grammar needs revising? What support are they likely to need, what is already available? Would a step-by-step writing frame be appropriate or would a range of questions be more useful?

SUMMARY

This chapter has attempted to outline the importance of developing reading and writing skills in pupils' modern FL learning. We have considered the use of writing frames and other support mechanisms and how technology can support the complex learning process. A range of examples are described to provide challenge and creativity to encourage pupils to engage in both reading and writing tasks.

REFERENCES

Atkinson, T. and Lazarus, E. (1997) *A Guide to Teaching Languages*. Cheltenham: MGP/ Stanley Thornes.

Erler, L. and Finkbeiner, C. (2007) 'A review of reading strategies: focus on the impact of first language', in Cohen, A. D. and Macaro, E. (eds), *Language Learner Strategies – Thirty Years of Research and Practice*. Oxford: Oxford University Press, pp. 229–250.

Gall, M., Lazarus, E., Tidmarsh, C. and Breeze, N. (2008) 'Creative designs for learning', in Sutherland, R., John, P. and Robertson, S. (eds), *Improving Classroom Learning through ICT*. London: Routledge, pp. 82–104.

Koda, K. (2005) *Insights into Second Language Reading – A Cross-Linguistic Approach*. Cambridge: Cambridge University Press.

Macaro, E. (2003) *Teaching and Learning a Second Language – A Review of Recent Research*. London/New York: Continuum.

Manchon, R. M., Roca de Larios, J. and Murphy, L. (2007) 'A review of writing strategies, focus on conceptualizations and impact of first language', in Cohen, A. D. and Macaro, E. (eds), *Language Learner Strategies – Thirty Years of Research and Practice*. Oxford: Oxford University Press, pp. 229–250.

Mitchell, R. and Myles, F. (1998) *Second Language Learning Theories*. London: Arnold.

Pachler, N., Evans, M., Redondo, A. and Fisher, L. (2014) *Learning to Teach Foreign Languages in the Secondary School*. London: Routledge.

Swarbrick, A. (1998) *More Reading for Pleasure in a Foreign Language, Pathfinder 36*. London: CILT.

WEBSITES

htttp://edublogs.org and http://blogger.com
http://qrcode.kaywa.com/ for generating QR codes
http://www.toondoo.com/ for creating comic strips
http://www.voki.com
http://www.wallwisher.com/ a bulletin board or wall to post ideas and comments on
http://www.wikispaces.com/ for creating wikis by teachers or pupils
http://wordle.net for creating interesting visuals, texts, books etc.

Chapter 8   Grammar in the foreign language classroom

LYNNE MEIRING AND NIGEL NORMAN

BY THE END OF THIS CHAPTER YOU SHOULD:

- have an understanding of the context and significance of grammar teaching in the foreign language (FL) classroom;
- understand the impact of policy on the teaching of grammar;
- understand the significance of grammar in developing literacy across the curriculum;
- be acquainted with some of the key issues and challenges relating to the teaching of grammar;
- be familiar with a sequenced approach to the teaching of grammar;
- be aware of a range of practical applications of grammar teaching.

SETTING THE SCENE

A panda walks into a café. He orders a sandwich, eats it, then draws a gun and fires two shots in the air.

'Why?' asks the confused waiter, as the panda makes towards the exit. The panda produces a badly punctuated wildlife manual and tosses it over his shoulder. 'I'm a panda,' he says, at the door. 'Look it up.'

The waiter turns to the relevant entry and, sure enough, finds an explanation. 'Panda. Large black-and-white bear-like mammal, native to China. Eats, shoots and leaves.'

(Truss, 2003)

- What can be learned from this story about the role of grammar and punctuation?
- What is their relationship with communication?

STATUS AND SIGNIFICANCE – WHY IS GRAMMAR IMPORTANT?

If vocabulary is the bricks and grammar the mortar, we can build a wall or a garage, a house or a castle. Just as a house without bricks would collapse, so too would it collapse without mortar. The mortar provides the disconnected bricks with meaning and purpose, a different purpose in each case, but the same mortar. Vocabulary without grammar has shape and meaning, but with grammar it has a unique purpose and definition – the user is empowered to build his own edifice with precision, detail, individuality and style. Take for example, the vocabulary items *car, hit, the, bus.* In this raw form, meaning is certainly conveyed. As soon as grammar is applied, the meaning can be changed for our own purposes. Thus, *The car was hit by the bus,* has significantly changed the meaning without adding any new vocabulary – it is the grammar, which has achieved this. In addition, grammar has the further advantage of assisting in the learning process by reducing the demands on memory. This is particularly important for the less able and Special Needs pupil, for whom the memory burden demanded by communicative language teaching methods is considerable.

GRAMMAR: ITS PLACE IN FL TEACHING

Traditionally the school curriculum in England and Wales has been largely determined by the requirements of public examinations. The National Curriculum, first introduced in 1988 (DfEE/QCA, 1999 and ACCAC/NAW, 2000), represents a further defining feature. A useful starting point in the consideration of grammar teaching would be to establish the place of grammar within the National Curriculum Orders, GCSE examinations and alternative courses.

Task 8.1

Reference to grammar in statutory documentation

Consult the National Curriculum for England or Wales, the current GCSE/A Level specifications and the current specifications for alternative courses, and track references, both direct and indirect, to grammar.

National Curriculum	GCSE/A Level	Alternative courses
e.g. Programme of Study 3.4 (ACCAC, 2000): 'pupils should be taught: the grammar of the target language, and how to apply it at a level appropriate to their ability.'	e.g. AQA 2004 Aims, French GCSE, Section 5c: 'this specification should encourage candidates to develop knowledge and understanding of the grammar of French, and the ability to apply it.'	e.g. International Baccalaureate, NVQ, Asset Languages e.g. Level 1, NVQ assessment criteria: 'be able to use a simple range of grammatical forms.'

A further significant development relating to the role of grammar is the increased emphasis on developing literacy across the curriculum. Grammar is a principal feature of all languages and, therefore, can inform language learning and literacy. Estyn (2009), cited in WG (2011), recommends that schools 'develop common practices between the English, Welsh and Modern Foreign Language departments to improve pupils' understanding of language concepts'. One of the purposes of the guidance in WG (2011) is to 'show how connections can be made to improve literacy in all languages.'

Task 8.2

Implications of grammatical features of lexical items

Make a list of words, which are similar or identical in English and in your Target Language (TL). Consider for each word the implications for teaching.

English	Target language	Implications for teaching
e.g. 'table	la table (French)	Pronunciation, gender

Task 8.3

Comparing grammar features across languages

List grammatical points in English, such as the Perfect Tense, and compare the formation and use with your TL. Identify how the English can support the teaching of the specific point (similarities and differences).

English	Target language	Similarities	Differences
'I played football...'	'Ich habe Fussball gespielt' (German)	Personal pronoun (Ich) Past participle (gespielt) Object (Fußball)	Auxiliary verb (habe) Word order of past participle (gespielt at end of sentence)

The National Literacy Strategy in England (DfEE, 1998) and subsequent National Literacy and Numeracy Framework in Wales (WG, 2013) also influenced the profile of grammar. This has played an important part in developing progression in language awareness, with its emphasis on words, sentences and texts. Building on this, the National Strategy Framework for teaching FL (DfES, 2003) shifted the emphasis from the teaching of grammar through topics (predominant in GCSE syllabuses) to a focus upon the language itself. Of the five strands that constituted the Framework, grammar was clearly embedded in two: words and sentences. Although these strategy documents no longer apply in England since 2011, they continue to be useful reference points.

KEY ISSUES AND CHALLENGES IN THE TEACHING OF GRAMMAR

Status of the target language (TL)

Is it feasible to teach grammar in the TL? If grammar is integral to language teaching, and an optimal use of the TL is desirable, this principle must surely be applied to the teaching of grammar. Yet there is a common perception that grammar, by virtue of its content, is intrinsically difficult for teacher and pupil in the TL. Possible reasons for this are the teachers' own lack of confidence in dealing with specialised vocabulary, and, as Meiring and Norman (2001, p. 64) point out: 'the conventions of coursebook practice have not been conducive to consistent TL teaching of grammar.' There is, however, a serious risk that if grammar is taught in

English it will be relegated to a 'different special and difficult category ... [thus] intimidating and impeding progress in learning.'

It appears, therefore, that it is the language that is causing the difficulty rather than the understanding of the concept. This applies to both teaching and learning. From a teaching perspective there is support available (see Macdonald, 1993), and for the learner understanding can be facilitated through the skilful use of appropriate visuals and other forms of support.

Task 8.4

Grammar explanations

Write a simple, but brief explanation in your TL for a Year 7 class of the difference between the 1st, 2nd and 3rd Person singular of the Present Tense of regular verbs.

If you were teaching this to a Year 7 class, suggest ways in which you might support the explanation, in order to remain teaching in the TL. What is the role of the mother tongue and of the TL in the explanation?

Stages of explanation	Support strategies

A further consideration in this debate is outlined by Butzkamm and Caldwell (2009), who make a case for the systematic use of the mother tongue to clarify meaning and grammar by means of the 'mirroring' technique. An example of this from the early stages of learning French is:

Je m'appelle
= My name is (clarifies the meaning)
=* I myself call (renders the structure transparent)

Therefore the judicious use of English in this case contributes to developing grammatical awareness, and clarifying linguistic misconceptions.

Task 8.5

'Mirroring'

Based on Butzkamm and Caldwell's (2009) 'mirroring' technique, create examples following the model below.

TL phrase	Clarification of meaning	Transparency of structure
J'apprends le français depuis deux ans	I have been learning French for two years	*I learn French since two years

---

Deductive or inductive approach?

Which comes first: rule or example? The deductive approach is based upon the rule followed by application of the rule in examples; the inductive approach introduces examples first from which the rule emerges. Both approaches have their place in a balanced teaching and learning environment. As early as 1632 Comenius stated: 'Children need to be given many examples and things they can see, and not abstract rules of grammar' (cited by Hawkins, 1994, p. 111). Yet he did not dismiss the contribution of a more explicit approach: 'rules assist and strengthen the knowledge derived from practice.' Some grammatical points lend themselves more to teacher explanation of the rule, followed by pupils' practice, whilst others would benefit more from presentation of examples by the teacher, with pupils working out the rule for themselves.

Further considerations in selecting an approach would be the age and ability of the learners and the time available. Clearly both deductive and inductive approaches should be seen as mutually supportive, and teachers might consider the most appropriate order according to circumstances. As Meiring and Norman state: 'pupils should be encouraged to induce rules of grammar themselves from a plethora of examples, and also to express these rules in their own words, which the teacher can then use as a basis for a more formal explanation' (Meiring & Norman, 2001, p. 63).

Task 8.6

Inductive and deductive approaches to grammar teaching

From the grammar of your TL, categorise six grammatical points that pupils would encounter in Key Stage 3. Consider whether the initial encounter with the grammar would be better served by an inductive or deductive teaching approach.

Inductive	Deductive

Consider in each case whether your opinion would change if you were teaching the same points to Key Stage 4 and at Advanced level, or according to the ability level of the class.

Technical terms

The National Literacy Strategy should have raised pupils' awareness of technical terms in their mother tongue, thus providing a basis for teachers to introduce the same concepts in the FL. In cases where pupils are not aware of the terms and concepts, this can be an obstacle to learning; where they *are* aware they are able to use dictionaries, glossaries etc. with greater ease, and progress is thus faster. The key to the use of technical terms is surely to use them in context, where they can be referred directly to the relevant language as it arises, and to avoid gratuitous use of over-complicated terms. The knowledge of technical terms has the potential to enable pupils to categorise new language, which will facilitate future retrieval, recycling and re-use. Pupils of all abilities benefit from this type of 'filing system', so that they can develop an ordered approach to what they learn. As Pachler,

Evans, Redondo and Fisher (2014, Chapter 11) state: 'By introducing new linguistic structures through unfamiliar terminology FLs teachers run the risk of pupils struggling with concepts at a level one step removed from the linguistic phenomenon itself' and 'Metalanguage can be introduced once a concept is understood by pupils.'

Task 8.7

Grammar terminology in the coursebook

Consult a Key Stage 3 coursebook and list the grammatical terms that pupils are likely to encounter. Find TL equivalents. How many of the terms are cognates?

English term	Example	Target language
e.g. possessive pronoun	mon, ma, mes	(pronom) possessif

Conceptual understanding

It is important to establish conceptual understanding of grammar from the early stages of learning a language, a process that could be described as 'concept planting'. It shares many of the characteristics of what has been called 'form-focused instruction', which is any planned or incidental instructional activity that is intended to induce the language learner to pay attention to linguistic form. Pachler, Evans, Redondo and Fisher (2014, Chapter 11) propose a sequence for the staged development of grammatical awareness from 'noticing' to 'integrating' to 'internalising' to 'proceduralising'. Thus learners notice or identify and label the language form, formulate a personal rule, linking it to previous knowledge, apply it and use it automatically through regular usage in a range of contexts.

The Verb Phrase, for example, demonstrates a complexity of features (e.g. variety of verb forms, tenses), but the principle of concept planting should still apply. Confusion often arises because, in the initial stages of language learning, a unit of words is taught lexically, rather than grammatically, e.g. j'ai douze ans, j'ai un frère. Pupils need to be taught, and thus show understanding, of the function of je/j', rather than to learn it by heart, as an item of vocabulary. This will enable them to recycle and transfer language in new contexts.

Task 8.8

Grammatical concepts at an early stage of learning

Suggest strategies for 'planting' the concept of the following grammatical points at an early stage of learning language. What grammatical points would be made more accessible through knowledge and understanding of gender and tense?

Gender (masc., fem., neuter)	Strategies & techniques for concept planting	Related grammatical points (e.g. prepositions)

Perfect Tense	Strategies & techniques for concept planting	Related grammatical points

Grammar and communication

An unfortunate consequence of communicative language teaching (CLT) has been the polarisation of grammar and communication at opposite ends of the pedagogical spectrum. In the context of the present-day classroom it is the position of grammar that has been marginalised. Yet communicative competence consists of four components (see Hymes, 1972), the first of which is grammatical competence. The setting of grammar and communicative approaches against one another in the classroom does a disservice to both; each have their place in a balanced approach.

As they stand, communicative syllabuses allow for relatively complex grammatical utterances to be used as chunks of language in phrase-book fashion. Thus, the first lesson of French commonly produces for example 'Comment t'appelles-tu?', a sentence that involves the question form and reflexive verb form, arguably a complex utterance to grasp structurally. It would be foolish to attempt to analyse the components of the utterance at this stage; however, it is useful to highlight such features as the personal pronoun and verb endings. This provides a starting point for raising awareness of language, which can be built upon subsequently. Turner (1995, p. 18) presents this as 'a spiral staircase ... which implies that grammatical items will come back round throughout the course. In other words, learners will gradually build up their knowledge of the grammatical system through the revisiting and extension of what has been covered in the past.' In this way the apparent mismatch between grammar and communication is a perceived, rather than an actual, difficulty, and both elements can be mutually supportive.

Task 8.9

Raising awareness of language forms

Consider the sentence 'Je voudrais aller au marché pour acheter un kilo de pommes.' Identify the separate grammatical features of the sentence and consider which ones you would emphasise to learners at an early stage to contribute towards raising their awareness of language forms.

Choose another sentence in your TL that contains a range of grammatical features, and analyse it in the same way.

Je voudrais aller au marché pour acheter un kilo de pommes.	Grammatical features (e.g. conditional)
.... (Your sentence)	....

Sequenced approach to the teaching of grammar

As we have established, the importance of a sequenced approach to the teaching of grammar is paramount. The role of the teacher is crucial in making 'a judicious selection of grammatical structures with a high indicator of usefulness and generative potential ... that will be useful in terms of transfer value' (Jones, 2000, pp. 146–147). A significant aspect of this is the recycling of previously acquired concepts. The danger of a topic-based approach is that the grammar will be confined to discrete units, dependent upon the topic content. Thus, at the beginning of each new unit of work a 'brainstorming' of the predicted language would enable the recycling of some items. Pachler, Evans, Redondo and Fisher (2014, Chapter 11) suggest that the selection of grammar should be based upon the following considerations:

- which items need to be 're-cycled' from previous units covered?
- which items meaningfully build on existing knowledge?
- which items should not be explained in full at this stage, but will require revisiting at a later stage?
- which items can be treated as lexical items at this stage?

In a topic based on shopping, pupils could conceivably determine that they would need to learn expressions of quantity. Such an approach empowers pupils, promotes thinking skills and motivates them through progression. It is important that linguistic recycling and spiralling becomes a practical reality.

Task 8.10

Recycling grammar points

Consider the topic of holidays in a Year 9 class under the following headings.

Recycled items	Existing knowledge	Grammatical items requiring explanation	Items to be taught lexically

PRACTICAL APPLICATIONS OF GRAMMAR TEACHING

Clearly, the issues raised above demand a range of strategies and resources. An over-riding recommendation must be that an integrated approach to grammar is adopted, rather than a 'bolt-on' approach in the mother tongue. The following are some examples of possible approaches, ranging from 'high tech'/state-of-the-art to 'no tech'/no frills:

'High tech':

- The interactive whiteboard allows pupils to manipulate words on screen effortlessly.
- Grammar software and websites enable repeated and individualised practice with instant, non-threatening feedback.
- The use of presentation software and interactive software enables the teacher to enhance presentational techniques, using the potential of graphics to clarify concepts.

'No tech':

- Colour-coded cards for the establishment and practice, for example, of gender and agreement.
- Timelines to establish the concept and use of tense.
- 'Washing lines' to illustrate and practise, for example, word order.

Use these suggestions as a basis for further activities.

Task 8.11

Strategies for presenting grammar

Following the examples given in the chapter, suggest other techniques and strategies for presenting grammar, and helping learners to understand concepts.

'High tech' strategies	'Low tech' strategies

For other practical suggestions see Rendall (1998), Neather (2003) and Biriotti (1999).

SUMMARY

It will be apparent from the discussion above that the issue of grammar in language teaching is both contentious and complex. Consideration has to be given to the impact of policy on practice. Nevertheless, teachers retain considerable autonomy in interpreting the demands of the curriculum. Having established in this chapter the importance of grammar, we have tried to suggest a reasoned approach consistent with prevailing communicative methodology. In so doing we have attempted to address some of the most contentious issues in grammar teaching, and shown the potential of an approach based upon recycling of previously acquired concepts, and that this contributes to the development of language awareness more effectively than a purely topic-based approach. Although we recognise the potential of new technologies in achieving this, much can be achieved through simple strategies.

The unnatural separation between grammar and communication in the past has clearly militated against a balanced approach to language learning. Integration of the two that recognises the role and potential of both will enable progression and enjoyment.

REFERENCES

ACCAC/National Assembly for Wales (2000) *Modern Foreign Languages in the National Curriculum in Wales.* Cardiff: ACCAC Publications.

Biriotti, L. (1999) *Grammar is Fun.* London: CILT.

Butzkamm, W. and Caldwell, J. A. W. (2009) *The Bilingual Reform. A Paradigm Shift in Foreign Language Teaching.* Tübingen: Gunter Narr Verlag.

DES/WO (1990) *Modern Foreign Languages for Ages 11 to 16.* London: HMSO.

DfEE/QCA (1999) *Modern Foreign Languages: The National Curriculum for England.* London: Department for Education and Employment, Qualifications and Curriculum Authority.

DfEE (1998) *The National Literacy Strategy. Framework for Teaching.* London: DfEE. Available at: http://webarchive.nationalarchives.gov.uk/20100612050234/http://nationalstrategies.standards.dcsf.gov.uk/primary/primaryframework

DfES (2003) *Key Stage 3 National Strategy. Framework for Teaching Modern Foreign Languages: Years 7, 8 and 9.* London: DfES. Available at: http://webarchive.nationalarchives.gov.uk/20110809101133/nsonline.org.uk/mfl

Estyn (2009) *Improving Modern Foreign Languages in Secondary Schools in Wales.* Cardiff: Estyn.

Hawkins, E. (1994) 'Percept before precept', in King, L. and Boaks, P. (eds) *Grammar! A Conference Report.* London: CILT, pp. 109–123.

Hymes, D. (1972) 'On communicative competence', in Pride, J. and Holmes, J. (eds), *Sociolinguistics: Selected Readings.* Harmondsworth: Penguin, pp. 269–293.

Jones, J. (2000) 'Teaching grammar in the modern foreign language classroom', in Field, K. (ed) *Issues in Modern Foreign Languages Teaching.* London: Routledge Falmer, pp. 142–157.

Macdonald, C. (1993) *Using the Target Language.* Cheltenham: Mary Glasgow Publications/A.L.L.

Meiring, L. and Norman, N. (2001) 'Grammar in MFL teaching revisited'. *Language Learning Journal* 23(1), 58–66.

Neather, T. (2003) *Getting to Grips with Grammar.* London: CILT.

Pachler, N., Evans, M., Redondo, A. and Fisher, L. (2014) *Learning to Teach Foreign Languages in the Secondary School.* 4th edition. London: Routledge.

Rendall, H. (1998) *Stimulating Grammatical Awareness. A Fresh Look at Language Acquisition.* London: CILT.

Truss, L. (2003) *Eats, Shoots and Leaves: The Zero Tolerance Approach to Punctuation.* London: Profile Books.

Turner, K. (1995) *Listening in a Foreign Language. A Skill We Can Take for Granted.* London: CILT.

WG (2011) *Supporting Triple Literacy. Language learning in Key Stage 2 and Key Stage 3*. Cardiff: Welsh Government.

WG (2013) *National Literacy and Numeracy Framework*. Cardiff: Welsh Government.

USEFUL WEBSITES

http://www.btinternet.com/~s.glover/S.Glover/languagesite/Default.htm
http://atschool.eduweb.co.uk/haberg/reallyusefulge/default.htm
http://www.quia.com/web
http://www.zut.org.uk/Home.html
http://web.uvic.ca/hrd/halfbaked/
http://www.linguascope.co.uk/

Chapter 9   The (inter)cultural turn in foreign language teaching

PRUE HOLMES

BY THE END OF THIS CHAPTER YOU SHOULD:

- recognise the importance of the (inter)cultural dimension of foreign language (FL) learning;
- understand the concepts of intercultural (communicative) competence and intercultural awareness and their role in the FL curriculum;
- be able to address the (inter)cultural dimension pedagogically and develop an intercultural dimension in learners.

INTRODUCTION

Since Byram, Gribkova and Starkey's (2002) publication 'Developing the Intercultural Dimensions of Language Teaching', the focus on the 'intercultural' in language teaching has strengthened further. The challenge for language teachers is to recognize and respond to this focus. Language learning policy and curricula now include the intercultural dimension of language teaching. But implementing this intercultural turn in their classrooms is not easy for language teachers, especially as governments and education ministries emphasise the need for teachers to meet school/national criteria in pupil performance. Further, language teachers themselves need to be interculturally aware, in terms of understanding their own culture and identity and their intercultural (communicative) competence, in order to successfully teach the intercultural dimension (see, for example, Sercu, 2005).

However, the focus in this chapter is not to explore how to develop teachers' intercultural competence, but rather, how teachers can develop it in their learners. Drawing on the liberal educational philosophy embodied in language teaching in the 19th century and characterised by Humboldt's notion of *Bildung*, Byram (2008, 2010) argues that language teachers – through their teaching of interculturality – are well placed to encourage learners to take action, together with others, and engage in democratic inquiry. According to the CEFR (Council of Europe, 2001, p. 3), language teaching is a means of ensuring that the population more widely can 'achieve a wider and deeper understanding of the way of life and forms of thought of other peoples and of their cultural heritage'. This broader aim can be achieved through developing in learners intercultural awareness, and developing their intercultural (communicative) competence (Byram, 1997).[1] The concepts embodied in intercultural competence include knowledge, attitudes, behaviours and (critical cultural) awareness – the ability to evaluate, critically and on the basis of explicit criteria, perspectives, practices and products in one's own and other cultures and countries. As such, the learner performs the role of intercultural mediator/speaker, someone who is aware of differences and similarities, is sensitive towards others and the culture in which they reside, and is also aware of his/her own (cultural) positioning, and as a result of this awareness, takes action.

Further, Levine and Phipps (2012) argue that language teachers need emergent and critical conceptual tools to move beyond 'a heavily skills-based approach". They advocate a critical approach to language pedagogy, which invites teachers and students to unpack, examine, contest and transform taken-for-granted assumptions that are ingrained in language programme direction, curricular and teaching practices.

With these goals in mind, three key challenges emerge:

- how to develop learners' intercultural communication and competence to enable them to manage intercultural encounters;
- how to build learners' identities so they can understand and know themselves in order to better know and understand others; and
- how to develop intercultural citizens who are able to take action against social injustice, inequality and misrepresentation in contexts of intercultural engagement.

In this chapter I attempt to address these challenges and present some examples of possible activities and pedagogies/approaches (e.g. online learning), which offer teachers ways of developing learners' intercultural understanding and competence. The approaches involve learners in experiential learning, and processes of comparison, analysis, reflection and cooperative action in order to build learners' intercultural capabilities in response to the intercultural turn.

IDENTITY AND CULTURE

A more recent intercultural turn in language education draws attention to the socially constructed nature of intercultural communication. First, learners need to understand the social and communicative processes that underpin constructions of culture and identity, and this entails that they understand their own identity and culture in order to understand others. This communicative view of language learning challenges essentialised and nationalistic views of culture – as in 'culture as a Big C' (through the study of national literatures, countries, histories, etc.) and the 'three Ps' (of products, practices and perspectives). Instead, there is a shift towards the 'five Cs' (context, cultures, comparisons, connections, communities) where language learning is focused on intercultural communication (US Universities National Standards of Foreign Language Education Project, 2006). Language learning is no longer about food, festivals, facts and flags, but understanding culture as a social construction: learners are encouraged to understand how culture – their own and that of others – permeates and shapes behaviour, interactions and language choices. It also requires an understanding of their own identity, and that of others, in this (intercultural) communicative process.

This conceptualisation of culture focuses on activity. Thus, if 'culture' is treated as a verb, that is, 'to culture' or 'to do Culture X', then its status changes from an entity to a process (Street, 1993; cited in Piller, 2011). Thus, Piller argues that an essentialist view of culture, which assumes that people in 'Culture X' behave in some predictable and preconceptualised way, is transformed into a social

PRUE HOLMES

constructionist one, which 'treats culture as something people do or which they perform' (p.15). For example, my stereotypical view that Finnish people use a lot of silence in communication is reconstructed when I engage in 'getting to know' conversation and information exchange and I realise that silence is not part of this activity, but that my interlocutor and I negotiate communication strategies of greeting and information sharing. We can say, then, that individuals, through their everyday situated communication with others, (re)construct and (re)negotiate their identities. This identity formation may be the result of communication among people in their own local group(s), or with people who are from other horizons (as in the case of my Finnish interlocutor and I). Cultural stereotypes of the other, a process described as 'otherising', while providing a starting point for understanding others, are contested and challenged in intercultural communication. I am left feeling that my cultural stereotype of Finnish people as 'quiet' and communing in silence is erroneous, unhelpful and inadequate.

Therefore, the language teacher's task is to find ways of encouraging students to recognise and confront stereotypes and quickly move beyond them. The following activity provides a way of exploring the complexity of identity, and hence, the limitations of stereotypes.

Task 9.1

Understanding complexity in identity

Ask your learners to analyse their own identity to understand its complexity, discussing their understanding in pairs (either providing a range of terms in the language of study, or asking students to identify the language required):

1   Write down your answer to these two questions: Who am I (i.e., how do I see myself; what identities do I portray to others)? How do others see me (i.e., what identities do others give to me)? Students can then discuss their answers in pairs.
2   Next, write down a list of all the different types of identities you can think of (e.g., family, national, linguistic, social, cultural, historical, personal, professional, local/regional, geographical, political, religious, racial, transnational/European/cosmopolitan, ethnic, hybrid, hyphenated, etc.).
3   Discuss your list with your partner's. Add any new identities and terms to your list.
4   Discuss the nature of these identities and how they differ, giving examples of each. Are there any others you can think of?
5   Which of the following words would you use to describe the nature of your identity? Static, expansive, flowing, definite, solid, finite, singular, blurry, fragmented, fluid, changing, linear, organic, fixed, bounded, multiple, unified, flexible.

You can follow up by explaining that identity labels like 'national/cultural identity,' 'individualist/collectivist' are problematic because they fix the identity of an individual, thus leading to essentialised understandings of others in a process known as 'otherisation' (Holliday, Hyde and Kullman, 2005).

As Hall, Evans and Nixon (2013) argue, how we project ourselves and the cultural identities we ascribe to ourselves have become more open-ended, variable and problematic, such that identities have become contradictory, continuously shift about and pull individuals in different directions. Chimamanda Adichie's 'Danger of a single story' narration on *YouTube* provides an excellent example of this Nigerian postcolonial writer's examination of her own experiences of being 'otherised' by non-Nigerians (http://youtu.be/D9Ihs241zeg).

In order to explore the concept of culture, teachers must construct tasks that engage learners in intercultural communication, which involves a process of comparison and contrast between their own socially constructed world and that of the other; learners reflect on knowledge of their own language and culture as well as that of the other. Cultural mapping enables learners to understand the complexity of their culture and identity beyond essentialised understandings of culture.

Task 9.2

Cultural mapping

1   Ask learners to plot the following on a piece of paper: who you are (name, origins, languages spoken); where you come/came from; what is important to you; who is important to you (now, from the past); how you see yourself; how others see you.

2   Next, ask learners to discuss how concepts of culture, history, politics, languages, power and context are present on their maps (either individually or in pairs). Looking back to the identity labels developed in Task 9.1 might be useful here. How have these representations changed over time?

3   Then ask them to consider how these concepts form their understanding of their own identity. To what extent might their cultural map influence how they communicate with others as they move in and out of different contexts and groups? (They may be able to make links to the dynamic nature of their own identity and cultural understanding as they consider these intercultural communicative processes.) Further, ask learners how communication channels (e.g., face to face, mediated, dialogic, virtual) influence how they communicate with others. Then follow up with an examination of the 'Iceberg' model of culture (http://www.docstoc.com/docs/22729585/Iceberg-Theory-of-Culture-Fine-Arts-Literature-Drama-Classical-Music-Folk-Dancing-Games-Cooking-Notions-of-Modesty-Conceptions-of-Beauty-Ideals-of-Governing-Rules-of-Descent-Child-Raising).

4   Ask learners to draw on the terms to find examples or representations of aspects of their own culture.

5   Thinking back to Task 9.1, ask learners to reflect on how static these terms are. In other words, do they always project these identities, or behave in these ways, or are there times when they prefer to disregard these unwritten rules of their culture? Do they know of others in their group/culture who disregard or abandon these values/behaviours? Why? In what ways are some of these behaviours being reconstructed and renegotiated over time/with influences of transnational movements and globalisation, etc.?

Together, Tasks 9.1 and 9.2 begin to illustrate to learners the extent to which identity and culture are complex and dynamic terms, and may be reconstructed and renegotiated as individuals engage in (intercultural) communication with others.

SELF, OTHER, LANGUAGE AND CULTURE IN THE INTERCULTURAL TURN: INTERCULTURAL ENCOUNTERS

In the act of intercultural communication (and learning), learners are engaged in interpreting self (intraculturality) and other (interculturality). Learners are expanding language through a process of languaging, which is dynamic, personal, expressive and creative, with no fixed boundaries (Shohamy, 2006; cited in Scarino, 2010). They tell stories of themselves and others, and theirselves are constructed by and through the various discourses that give meaning to their lives, beyond the dualities of national languages (L1–L2) and national cultures (C1–C2). As Kramsch (2011) argues, this communication of the symbolic self, 'the most sacred part of our personal and social identity, … demands for its well-being careful positioning, delicate facework, and the ability to frame and re-frame events' (p. 354).

Kramsch (2011) argues that 'this symbolic dimension of intercultural competence calls for an approach to research and teaching that is discourse-based, historically grounded, aesthetically sensitive, and that takes into account the actual, the imagined and the virtual worlds in which we live' (p. 354). For example, online learning tools enable learners to engage in online or face to face interactions where they can construct 'their own and others' subject positions through the questions they ask and the topics they choose to talk about or to avoid' (Kramsch, 2013, p. 68).[2] Intercultural communication activities must therefore reflect learning about oneself – self identity – as much as about others' identities.

Language learning activities are beginning to reflect this approach, in particular, in a growing shift towards intercultural encounters as the focus of intercultural competence development (Barrett, Byram, Lázár, Mompoint-Gaillard and Philippou, 2013). Intercultural encounters take place when two or more people interact in situations where they perceive each other to have different cultural backgrounds or come from different horizons – they are from different countries, regions, religions, ethnicities – and when these differences are salient and affect the nature of the interaction (Barrett *et al.*, 2013). They involve a delicate process of 'face work' and identity negotiation. They also involve processes of preparation, engagement, evaluation of performance (one's own and that of the other) and reflection in an ongoing cyclical process (Holmes, 2010; 2012).[3] The following activity facilitates this process of intercultural learning.

> ### Task 9.3
>
> #### Autobiography of intercultural encounters
>
> The Autobiography of Intercultural Encounters (AIE) (Council of Europe, 2009) is a widely recognised, useful tool in developing learners' awareness of self in relation to the other, encouraging learners to think about both differences and similarities between themselves and their interlocutor and, importantly, inviting them to consider what action may result from the encounter. The activity is informed by theories of intercultural competence (namely, that of Byram, 1997). The description of key terms and concepts underpinning intercultural communication (available on the AIE website http://www.coe.int/t/dg4/autobiography/default_en.asp) enables teachers to introduce language learners to the important concepts of intercultural communication in intercultural encounters. The AIE has two ready-to-use formats, one for adults and one for younger learners. The AIE takes learners through a series of prompts, inviting them to describe the context of the encounter, who said what to whom, when

and where; the prompts also invite learners to reflect on the encounter – how they felt about the encounter, how the other experienced the encounter, and what action they will take, if at all, as a result of the encounter.

The AIE is complemented by the 'Autobiography of Intercultural Encounters through Visual Media' (AIEVM), designed to establish how visual media (e.g., television, the Internet, film, photography, drama, street theatre, art, etc.) create in people an awareness of otherness. The AIEVM is a welcome addition to so-defined 'monolingual' learning contexts where there appears to be less opportunity for overt intercultural communication in the community.

PEDAGOGIES OF ONLINE LEARNING TO FACILITATE THE DEVELOPMENT OF INTERCULTURAL COMPETENCE

Pedagogies of online learning, or telecollaboration, are opening up further opportunities for teachers to engage learners across regions and countries in authentic, purposeful and (a)synchronous intercultural exchange. Many secondary schools have benefited from networks such as etwinning (http://www.etwinning. net) and ePals (http://www.epals.com/) to bring learners into contact with partner classes. The following two studies provide specific examples that illustrate the potential for teachers and learners.

Example 1: Intercultural communication across four European countries

Lázár (2014) describes a collaboration among teachers in four European countries that involves learners in telecollaboration over five months. In mixed teams they discussed and reflected on a variety of topics in order to get to know each other's multiple perspectives: for example, typical meals and table manners; selecting, discussing and then translating popular songs; presenting themselves and their cities. The online platform, MOODLE, was used to upload texts, pictures and documents; and MOODLE resources such as discussion forums, journals, wikis and live chat sessions supplemented the pedagogy. The outcomes indicated improved intercultural competence by the end of the project, with the majority of the students feeling that they benefited from working together online.

Example 2: Developing culture-general awareness in a monolingual/ monocultural classroom via wikis

A further example involves the use of a wiki project to develop general cultural awareness (Trejo and Fay, 2013). Less ambitious in its aims, this project draws on the use of wikis among learners in the monolingual context of a Mexican classroom. Trejo and Fay used critical incidents as the prompt for student engagement, but teachers could also use problematic dialogues, scenarios, case studies, etc. They invited their learners to engage in the following seven steps:

• post reactions to and reflections on the issues presented in the critical incidents;
• brainstorm topics for further research (in the TL) related to the critical incident (e.g., one group explored practices around marriage proposals in Iran to find out how a British male might inform his Iranian fiancé's father of their marriage intentions);

81

- use the outcomes of this research to revisit initial responses and to further discuss them collectively;
- publish their responses on the wiki;
- form groups to further share ideas via the wiki;
- present their group understanding to other groups; and finally,
- as a class, explore the issues as they might play out in the Mexican context.

These two examples illustrate the enjoyment learners derived from meaningful engagement via technology, in both intercultural and monocultural/monolingual contexts.

FURTHER METHODS/APPROACHES TO DEVELOPING INTERCULTURAL (COMMUNICATIVE) COMPETENCE

In addition to telecollaboration, there are a variety of other approaches and pedagogies that have been developed by teachers and researchers and embedded in learner experience, to develop learners' intercultural (communicative) competence. (Some of these approaches have been summarised from Barrett *et al.* (2013) and are explained in more detail there.)

CLIL

The adoption of content language and integrated learning (CLIL) is developing in Europe, and offers opportunities for intercultural learning and engagement. Marsh and Langé (2000, p. 1; cited in Byram, 2008) describe CLIL as 'a generic term [which] refers to any educational situation in which an additional language, and therefore not the most widely used language of the environment, is used for the teaching and learning of subjects other than the language itself'.

The following four concepts that embody CLIL suggest ways of building intercultural competence through language:

- *content* – progression in knowledge, skills and understanding related to specific elements of a defined curriculum (i.e., culture learning through history, geography, literature, languages);
- *communication* – using language to learn while learning to use language;
- *cognition* – developing thinking skills which link concept formation (abstract and concrete), understanding and language, (e.g., via the five *savoirs* in Byram's intercultural competence model); and
- *culture* – exposure to alternative perspectives and shared understandings which deepen awareness of otherness and self (e.g., through intercultural interaction) (adapted from Byram, 2008).

To this end, Byram is leading a project, where a network of teachers (belonging to Durham University's Cultnet) are producing language learning activities that combine a CLIL classroom concept with a citizenship education model designed to develop learners' civic responsibility, action taking skills and intercultural competence (in particular, critical cultural awareness). The outcome is a proposed book publication which will be a valuable resource for language teachers.

Activities that invite multiple perspectives

These activities invite learners to discuss their own and the other's perspective in a process of decentring, and comparison and contrast, followed by further reflection and possibly action. Stories and biographies are useful here in enabling learners to consider how diversity, and social and historical contexts of individuals' experience influenced events and trajectories in their lives. Maps showing different projections enable learners to discuss viewpoints that are commonly accepted and those less customary.

Role plays, simulations and drama

These enable learners to take on new identities as they solve a problem, carry out a task or discuss an issue according to the norms of the assumed role. Learners can experience first-hand strangeness, criticism and exclusion. Post-discussion enables learners to experience marginalisation and difference, and deconstruct stereotypes about and ethnocentric positions towards others.

Films, texts, theatre, poetry and creative writing

Watching films and plays and reading plays, poems and other texts, allows learners to learn about people they have never met and lives they have never imagined. Through creative writing they can reconstruct the narrative from their own perspective. Such activities can prompt reconsideration of taken-for-granted attitudes and stereotypes, and even encourage learners to understand how society can protect the dignity and human rights of people with whom they might never have contact.

Ethnography

Learners can conduct 'fieldwork' outside the classroom by recording (using an observation grid) verbal and non-verbal communication of others, and explore how people express emotions such as respect, gratitude, anger. Learners can also 'interview' other community members and neighbours to find out their perspectives on community issues. Learners can compare and contrast results in the classroom, reflecting on their own values, attitudes and communication skills.

Social media (chat rooms, public fora), teleconferencing and online tools

Carefully moderated and guided, these tools offer learners opportunities to engage in real time communication and also expose their own 'voice'. Facilitated and guided reflection can help learners to consider their own attitudes, perspectives, and even miscommunication, when faced with ambiguity, and to confront these through experience of and reflection on their intercultural communication with another. O'Dowd's (2007) book provides a useful exploration of how teachers can use telecollaboration with their learners. And Develotte and Leeds-Hurwitz (2014) explore the use of online technologies in constructing conditions for intercultural dialogue between language teachers and learners.

ASSESSMENT

A final brief mention is necessary regarding assessment. How and whether to assess intercultural competence remains a contentious issue with no clear-cut resolutions. Educational regimes require that learning is assessed, and learners are assessment driven in their choices about whether and what to learn. Attempts to manage assessment have been addressed through the development of scales (e.g., INCA, CEFR) and inventories (e.g., FREPA/CARAP) of intercultural competence, which are readily available for teachers' use on the respective websites. Scarino (2010) raises several problems in trying to assess intercultural competence, or using her term, 'intercultural capabilities': how can it be assessed when it involves values? What constitutes evidence of its development? How do teachers judge it? Should it be assessed? She suggests an interpretive/meaning making approach which includes an ongoing process of enquiry, of data gathering and analysis of teachers' and learners' understandings of learners' learning, and that each teaching/learning experience affords teachers and learners with another experience to better understand the complexity of teaching, learning and assessing intercultural competence.

However, in the current secondary school context, assessment still remains a challenging task for teachers.

IMPLICATIONS AND CONCLUSIONS

The complexity of developing intercultural competence in learners, and the wide variety of approaches and pedagogies available, offer potential for language teachers in the classroom. Theoretical developments in intercultural competence and intercultural education for citizenship highlight the limitations of approaches that reify culture as knowledge of facts, food, festivals and flags. As I have illustrated, such knowledge is unhelpful in enabling individuals to:

1 engage in real-time communication, whether in their own language or in that of another person;
2 interpret and understand others' behaviours, communication and interactions; and/or
3 solve (intercultural communication) problems.

The goals implied in these new directions may seem ambitious within the context of the language classroom as learners grapple with developing linguistic knowledge and communicative competence. They raise significant and important challenges for language teachers.

However, teachers, too, can contribute to understandings and processes of developing intercultural communication and competence in their learners. By examining their assumptions and reflecting on practice, they can theorise about their own language pedagogy/learning as they respond to the intercultural turn. (For examples of teacher-led research see the special issue edited by Byram, Holmes and Savvides, 2013; Hawkins, 2011; Tsau and Houghton, 2010; Witte and Harden, 2011).

Moreover, not all learners' everyday experiences are characterised by post-modernity; language teachers must also find methods of developing intercultural competence within contexts that are seemingly monolingual/monocultural, yet simultaneously prepare learners for likely intercultural engagement in the future.

NOTES

1 Language teachers can read more about practical guidelines and tools for implementing this aim in the Council of Europe's (2010) document *Guide for the development and implementation of curricula for plurilingual and intercultural education* by Jean-Claude Beacco, Michael Byram, Marisa Cavalli, Daniel Coste, Mirjam Egli Cuenat, Francis Goullier and Johanna Panthier (Language Policy Division), http://www.coe.int/t/dg4/linguistic/Source/Source2010_ForumGeneva/GuideEPI2010_EN.pdf

2 See Kramsch (2013) for a review of the development of the concept 'culture' in language education.

3 These two studies describe a pedagogy of intercultural encounters and how to develop learners awareness and processes of evaluation of their own intercultural competence through the ongoing cyclical process, drawing on the PEER (prepare, engage, evaluate, reflect) model.

REFERENCES

Barrett, M., Byram, M.S., Lázár, I., Mompoint-Gaillard P. and Philippou, S. (2013) *Developing Intercultural Competence Through Education*. Strasbourg: Council of Europe.

Byram, M. S. (1997) *Teaching and Assessing Intercultural Communicative Competence*. Clevedon: Multilingual Matters.

Byram, M. S. (2008) *From Foreign Language Education to Education for Intercultural Citizenship*. Clevedon: Multilingual Matters.

Byram, M. S. (2010) 'Linguistic and cultural education for *Bildung* and citizenship'. *The Modern Foreign Language Teacher*, 94(2), 317–321.

Byram, M. S., Gribkova, B., and Starkey, H. (2002) *The Intercultural Dimensions of Language Teaching: A Practical Introduction for Teachers*. Strasbourg: Council of Europe.

Byram, M. S., Holmes, P. and Savvides, N. (2013) 'The intercultural dimensions of language teaching' [Special Issue]. *Language Learning Journal*, 41(3), 251–253.

Council of Europe (2001) *Common European Framework of Reference for Languages: Learning, Teaching, Assessment*. Strasbourg: Language Policy Unit. Available at: http://www.coe.int/t/dg4/linguistic/source/framework/en.pdf

Council of Europe (2009) *Autobiography of Intercultural Encounters*. Strasbourg: Language Policy Division.

Develotte, C. and Leeds-Hurwitz, W. (2014) '*Le Français en (premiere) ligne*: Creating contexts for intercultural dialogue in the classroom', in Haydari, N. and Holmes, P. (eds), *Case Studies in Intercultural Dialogue*. Dubuque, IA: Kendall-Hunt.

Hawkins, (2011) *Social Justice Language Teacher Education*. Clevedon: Multilingual Matters.

Hall, S., Evans, J. and Nixon, S. (2013) *Representation: Cultural Representations and Signifying Practices*. 2nd edition. London: Sage.

Holliday, A., Hyde, M. and Kullman, J. (2005) *Intercultural Communication: An Advanced Resource*. London: Sage.

Holmes, P. (2010) 'Autoethnography and self-reflection: Tools for self-assessing intercultural competence', in Tsau, J. and Houghton, S. (eds), *Becoming Intercultural: Inside and Outside the Classroom* (pp. 167–193). Newcastle upon Tyne: Cambridge Scholars.

Holmes, P. (2012) 'Developing and evaluating intercultural competence: Ethnographies of intercultural encounters'. *International Journal of Intercultural Relations*, 36(5), 707–718.

Kramsch, C. (2011) 'The symbolic dimensions of the intercultural'. *Language Teacher*, 44(3), 354–367.

Kramsch, C. (2013) 'Culture in foreign language teaching'. *Iranian Journal of Language Teaching Research*, 1(1), 57–78.

Lázár, I. (2014) 'EFL learners' intercultural competence development in an international web collaboration project'. *The Language Learning Journal*. Online. DOI: 10.1080/09571736. 2013.809941.

Levine, G. and Phipps, A. (2012) *Critical and Intercultural Theory and Language Pedagogy.* Boston, MA: Heinle, Cengage Learning.

Marsh, D. and Langé, G. (2000) *Using Languages to Learn and Learning to Use Languages.* Jyväskylä and Milan: TIE-CLIL.

O'Dowd, R. (2007) *Online Intercultural Exchange: An Introduction for Foreign Language Teachers.* Clevedon: Multilingual Matters.

Piller, I. (2011) *Intercultural Communication: A Critical Introduction.* Edinburgh: Edinburgh University Press.

Scarino, A. (2010) 'Assessing intercultural capability in learning languages: A renewed understanding of language, culture, learning and the nature of assessment.' *The Modern Language Journal,* 94(2), 324–328.

Sercu, L. (2005) *Foreign Language Teachers and Intercultural Competence.* Clevedon: Multilingual Matters.

Trejo, P. and Fay, R. (2013) 'Developing general cultural awareness in a monocultural English as a foreign language context in a Mexican university: A wiki-based critical incident approach'. *The Language Learning Journal*. Online. DOI: 10.1080/09571736.2013. 858549.

Tsau, J. and Houghton, S. (eds) (2010) *Becoming Intercultural: Inside and Outside the Classroom.* Newcastle upon Tyne: Cambridge Scholars.

US Universities National Standards of Foreign Language Education Project (2006) Available at: http//www.actfl.org/advocacy/discover-languages/advocacy/discover-languages/advocacy/discover-languages/resources-1?pageid=3392.

Witte, A. and Harden, T. (eds) (2011) *Intercultural Competence: Concepts, Challenges, Evaluations.* Bern: Peter Lang.

Chapter 10 Supporting foreign language learning through homework

MARILYN HUNT

BY THE END OF THIS CHAPTER YOU SHOULD:

- understand the reasons for setting homework;
- have gained an insight into the benefits of homework to teaching and learning;
- have considered different types of homework, including the use of ICT;
- have reflected on the setting of homework within a lesson and what constitutes a valid homework activity;
- recognise how homework links into assessment for learning.

REASONS FOR SETTING HOMEWORK

Homework continues to be an issue for debate by pupils, parents and teachers. Is it unnecessary educational overtime or an essential extra-curricular activity? You might like to consider where you stand in the homework debate before reading this chapter and reconsider your views at the end and especially after your experiences in school.

It would be useful to start by looking at a definition of homework, or home learning as it is often referred to now, used by one secondary school:

> Home learning encompasses all learning that takes place outside of the taught classroom environment; typically it will happen at home, but it might be completed in the Learning Resource Centre, a public library, or other suitable environment. Home learning should be varied and enjoyable, using a full range of 21st century media, including books, magazines, newspapers, Internet, social media, photography, television, radio and film.

Already this gives a positive view of homework, emphasising variety, enjoyment and the use of a full range of media. Yet in your placement schools you will come across a diversity of school homework policies. In some schools there are strict homework policies with timetables and allocated number of minutes for each subject on specific days. In other schools there are longer extended homework projects and in others a policy of no homework at all.

The latter situation is somewhat surprising as non-statutory homework guidelines were published by the DfES in 1998, and by September 1999 all schools in England were obliged to have a home–school agreement on homework. Although the agreement was not legally binding, it was considered to be a declaration of intent on the part of the school, the parent and the child. At the time of writing, guidance from the Department for Education no longer sets out how much homework children should get and, instead, allows a school to make its own decisions.

BENEFITS OF HOMEWORK TO TEACHING AND LEARNING

Although a minority view homework as unnecessary, potentially disadvantageous to schools and detrimental to students and their families (Cowan and Hallam, 1999), the majority of teachers, researchers and commentators regard homework as highly beneficial to teaching and learning and an essential component of school education. So what are the benefits?

Task 10.1

The benefits of homework

Before reading this section, reflect on the benefits of homework in general and consider specifically how homework benefits foreign language learning.

Firstly, homework allows further practice and consolidation of work covered in class time. This can extend learning, challenge understanding and allow students to try out new learning styles and contexts. This is especially important in language learning as knowledge of vocabulary and structures is essential to progress. For example, Ofsted (2002) reported:

> As a consequence of good planning, lesson time is used fully for learning and this is supported in turn by conscientiously done homework. Thus, pupils' grasp and retention of vocabulary and structure are strong and teachers can move on to more demanding tasks without backtracking to plug gaps in knowledge.

Homework also allows students to prepare for future classwork, for example by learning vocabulary or preparing a dialogue to act out. By providing opportunities for independent private study, homework can help students to gain independent learning skills, improving enquiry, investigative and research skills, self-discipline and time management, prioritization and organisational skills. Home learning can offer access to resources which may not be available in school so that students can develop skills in using library and other learning resources, including a full range of media. Again this is especially helpful for language learning as it can provide access to authentic target language (TL) materials. For the students, home learning can provide opportunities for individualised work and can develop confidence and promote creativity. For teachers, homework provides opportunities to support students through differentiated tasks and allows assessment of students' progress, providing feedback on learning difficulties and evidence for evaluation of teaching. Finally, homework can provide opportunities for parental co-operation and support and create channels for home–school dialogue. Home learning activities and tasks that are accessible on the school website or Virtual Learning Environment (VLE) enable parents and carers to be more involved and engaged in their child's learning.

TYPES OF HOMEWORK

REFLECTIONS OF PERSONAL EXPERIENCE AND PRACTICE

Think about your experiences so far in setting or seeing homework set. Is it set appropriately and regularly according to agreed procedures? What types of homework are set?

Homework can take a variety of forms but you will probably find learning and written exercises predominate. This need not be the case. There is ample scope for developing skills in addition to expanding linguistic knowledge through investigation/research; project type work; reading work; listening tasks; speaking tasks and computer-based activities. Even writing tasks can vary from directed to open tasks. The challenge is to plan homework which is relevant to the learning objectives and extends or consolidates the learning, but which is also motivating for students. Providing a choice of tasks, perhaps related to different levels, is one way of developing student autonomy. It is also important to tailor it to the needs of the students in your class, possibly with differentiated must/should/could tasks so that homework is within the ability of pupils, but provides opportunity for challenge so that all pupils can achieve something. Planning homework thus needs to be part of the overall planning process for lessons and modules/units of work. Maintaining a record of homework set for each class can ensure students enjoy a variety of types of homework so that interest level is sustained. Homework can be pupil-initiated and/or pupil-led.

Alternative/more unusual types of homework:

- ask the pupils to summarise a grammar point;
- list five ways of memorising vocabulary?
- look up words in the dictionary?
- read a text and annotate it with words related to English/which they know/ which they don't know etc.;
- write in English the phrases they feel would be crucial in a particular context;
- design a colourful mind map of useful connectives, adjectives and opinion phrases;
- list useful verbs connected to a topic, for example free time, in 3 tenses;
- prepare a spoken presentation;
- submit homework as an email attachment;
- personalise some homework tasks to pupils' interests;
- set 'tangible' homework sometimes, e.g. where pupils have to bring something in;
- relate a homework task to celebrities or a favourite TV programme.

The use of Information and Communication Technologies (ICT) has widened the range of homework possibilities. Many schools have intranets with language specific tasks or subscriptions to websites which students can use to practise vocabulary or grammar items. Tasks of a more interactive nature include posting messages, for example questions, comments, thoughts, like virtual post-it notes on a wall (http://padlet.com/). Some teachers are making innovative use of wikis, blogs and social media, although clearly e-safety needs to be paramount. One idea for a blog is to encourage pupils to up-load their work and set a peer assessment task where each student has to comment on five others' pieces of work, giving positive comments and offering suggestions of ways to improve. This is all exciting, as it can make the homework interactive and more relevant to the learners.

Long-lasting homework tasks are also used in some schools in addition to, or instead of, shorter weekly tasks. Pupils are expected to work on this over time or when homework may be difficult to set, for example because of staff absence. A choice of tasks is given devised to suit all abilities, and this element of choice is generally found to be motivating.

Task 10.3

Differentiating homework across year groups

Think about how homework changes in different year groups and why.

PUPILS' HOMEWORK PREFERENCES

An action research project (Hunt, Barnes and Redford, 2009), developed between teacher educators and a FLs department in a specialist language college, aimed to create stimulating homework tasks based on Year 9 pupils' views. Baseline attitudes and information were sought through a pupil questionnaire to establish pupils' homework preferences and a staff questionnaire to discover their views on homework, the types of tasks they set and to ascertain any problems with homework in Year 9. The types of tasks pupils liked included creativity, research, using ICT and more extended project-style work. Responding to these views, a six-week homework project was devised with a collaborative element and an end product (leaflet/brochure/interactive display) to send to pen-pal links. Pupils responded positively and appreciated the sense of ownership and purpose; they enjoyed collaborative work with a partner and the fact that their work had a special audience other than their teacher.

Task 10.4

Pupils' homework preferences

Look at the pupils' comments at the end of the project. Consider how you might devise a similar action research project to ascertain your own pupils' homework preferences and respond to them to increase the effectiveness of languages homework.

'You can go home and write at your own pace and be more creative with your ideas.'

'It's different; normally we just do sheets and can't be bothered to do it, but working with a partner and on the computer it's more interesting.'

'It's boring in Year 7 and 8 'cos it's always 'finish off ....' but this time every step you take you learn something new.'

SETTING HOMEWORK WITHIN A LESSON

Planning homework is a vital part of your lesson planning. You will need to check the school and department homework policy as you will need to follow whatever system is used. Is there a homework schedule, where French/German/Spanish can only be set on certain nights? Do pupils at your school have a homework diary? Once you have determined this framework you will need to make a series of decisions each time you plan a lesson:

- what homework to set;
- at which point in the lesson you will set homework;
- clear instructions of your expectations;
- and a range of types of homework over time.

Homework tasks may be written into the scheme of work or you may need to devise your own. In either case it is important to provide an appropriate activity building on work done in the lesson. It is pointless giving homework activities to do in class and trivial things to do at home! Homework also needs to be achievable. Is the homework still going to be appropriate if your planned lesson activities are not completed?

The point at which you set homework needs to be considered carefully. Setting early in the lesson may mean you have pupils' attention, but equally it uses the most beneficial learning time. Setting at the end of a lesson may mean you run out of time. Ensure that you formulate in detail in advance what is expected of your pupils. Choose a point between learning tasks and, when setting homework, give clear instructions and a demonstration. Back up homework instructions with written instructions on the board, ensure students use their homework diary properly and check that students understand the task.

Following up homework is essential. Firstly there are the practicalities of deciding when to collect in homework: at the beginning of the lesson or leave on the desk at the end? When you take their books in, will they be able to do the next homework you set? Providing feedback on homework, whether by testing learning homework or speaking presentations in class or marking and returning work with comments and rewards where deserved, are all important in developing learning. Common mistakes in homework may tell you something about your teaching or the task and these can be used for teaching points in future lessons.

VALID HOMEWORK ACTIVITIES

Whilst you may be required to set homework to meet school policy, homework should not just be given for the sake of it. Put yourself in the position of the pupils – would *you* want to do this homework, or are you just setting it because you have to? The potential for stimulating and varied homework has been mentioned earlier. Two omissions were pointed out by Ofsted (2008: 15): 'Generally, the potential of homework for students to practise reading for pleasure and writing at length was not realised'.

Task 10.5

Validity of homework activities

Consider the following homework activities. Are they valid? How could they be improved?

- 'Make sure you know all the vocabulary we did today'.
- 'Write out a conversation with your partner for homework'.
- 'Start this now and what you don't finish in class, you can do for homework'.

HOW HOMEWORK LINKS INTO ASSESSMENT FOR LEARNING

Your day-to-day records of homework set and marks achieved will form part of your records of pupil progress along with pupils' performance in class tasks, tests or end of unit activities. Schools may use a system of codes as below:

Abs = absent when homework set
A = absent when homework collected in
L = late homework
U = unfinished homework
X = homework not done/targets not achieved

To support self-assessment you could encourage pupils to check certain elements before handing in their homework. For example, in German:

Check that you have used the correct verb endings:

✓ ich = e/er and sie = t

Then check the following:

Your nouns have a capital letter

✓ Your verbs have a small letter
✓ A (masc = einen/fem = eine/neut = ein)
✓ The (masc = den/fem = die/neut = das)

Task 10.6

Homework self-assessment checklist

Devise checklists for French/Spanish/German for different year groups.

All home learning tasks should be completed and handed in on time and to a standard acceptable to the classroom teacher (reflecting the age and ability of the pupils). Likewise, homework should be marked and returned to pupils with feedback on strengths and targets to help learning progress. Assessing homework will help to evaluate your teaching and pupils' learning and will feed into your future planning.

Where a pupil misses a deadline or hands in work below the acceptable standard you will need to follow school policy on sanctions.

SUMMARY

At first all new teachers find the planning and assessment of homework a laborious and time-consuming process, but it can be an invaluable tool to extend and consolidate learning and provide feedback to both teachers and students on what has been achieved and what needs to be done next to develop learning.

REFERENCES

Cowan, R. and Hallam, S. (1999) *What Do We Know About Homework? Viewpoint 9.* London: Institute of Education, University of London.

DfES (1998) *Homework: Guidelines for Primary and Secondary School.* London.

Hunt, M., Barnes, A. and Redford, J. (2009) 'MFL homework in year 9 French: rising to the challenge'. *Language Learning Journal* 37(1), 35–49.

Ofsted (2002) *Good Teaching, Effective Departments.* London. Available at http://www.ofsted. gov.uk/resources/good-teaching-effective-departments

Ofsted (2008) *The Changing Landscape of Languages.* London. Available at http://www.ofsted. gov.uk/resources/changing-landscape-of-languages

Chapter 11   Digital technologies in foreign language teaching and learning

THOMAS STRASSER AND NORBERT PACHLER

BY THE END OF THIS CHAPTER YOU SHOULD:

- have an appreciation of the potential of internet-based tools and services for foreign language (FL) teaching and learning;
- have a conceptual and practical understanding of the explorative, collaborative, interactive and participatory approaches to FL teaching and learning digital technologies afford.

INTRODUCTION

In the age of the internet, phenomena such as Web 2.0, social media and digital technologies, in particular browser-based applications, tools and services as well as mobile devices, have played a considerable role also in the field of FL teaching and learning in recent years (see e.g. Buchberger *et al.*, 2011). In the space available here it is not possible to do justice to the myriad of possibilities stretching from the use of (digital) audio and video recording, computer-assisted language learning (CALL) software, such as text manipulation programs, to delayed- (asynchronous) and real-time (synchronous) computer mediated communication such as e-mail, chat and audio- and video-conferencing or various virtual learning environments, such as Moodle or Blackboard, or ePortfolio-applications, such as Mahara. In order to avoid a superficial treatment of the wide-ranging field of internet-based tools or applications, we focus here on certain characteristics of what we call browser-based 'Educational Applications'. By this we do not mean educational 'apps' on the App Store or on Google Play but rather online tools and services, which have gained importance especially in FL teaching (see e.g. Strasser, 2012a or http://bit. ly/tools-tag).

This chapter builds on and complements aspects of the use of educational technology covered in *Learning to Teach Foreign Languages in Secondary School* (Pachler, Evans, Redondo and Fisher, 2014) with particular reference to didactically versatile and technologically simple technologies, so that you will be able to focus on the learning outcomes of your pupils, rather than on technical challenges, with the aim of enriching and enhancing your personal and your pupils' learning experience.

THE ROLE OF TEACHERS AND LEARNERS AS ACTIVE PARTICIPANTS

The role of the teacher in the context of technology-enhanced language learning can be considered important when it comes to providing instruction, initiating social connectedness and offering technical support (see e.g. Chang, 2004). However, many observers note that there has been an explicit shift from the teacher as instructor or sole expert towards a coach or facilitator actively collaborating with the pupils, who in turn bring in their own technical expertise (see e.g. Schiefner and Kerres, 2011; Wiley and Hilton, 2009; Dinevski and Arh, 2012). Using tools such as wikis, forums, blogs, podcasting or cartoon applications, teachers and pupils can profit from each other by working collaboratively and interactively on artefacts, e.g. 'composing' (multimodal) texts (see e.g. Bachmair and Pachler, 2013). Just as the role of the teacher changes from being mainly an instructor, so does that of the pupil from being a relatively passive recipient in a transmission and delivery paradigm of teaching to becoming an active member of a communicative and collaborative process. In this paradigm of learning (as semiotic 'work' around meaning making) (see e.g. Kress and Pachler, 2007), digital technologies become powerful tools for explorative, collaborative and highly interactive learning, allowing pupils to construct new knowledge and understand certain curricular aspects through a more participatory approach. Therefore, it can be noted that due to a 'de-verticalized hierarchy' (i.e. teachers and pupils both acting as participants in a virtual learning scenario; see Strasser, 2012b), they complement one another with their respective expertise in technology-related and subject-specific (language learning-related) fields. Considering the fact that in traditional classroom settings the teacher still often acts as an instructor or knowledge-provider (see e.g. Cole and Foster, 2008), constructivist learning approaches within a digital technology-rich context (i.e. characterised by the use of internet-based tools) allow pupils and teachers to work independently, autonomously and collaboratively with a wide range of resources as well as within teams. In this respect, the teacher experiences a shift from the 'master' towards a 'communicative collaborator' who is not the only source of knowledge within technology-rich and distributed learning contexts. Within such a paradigm of learning, digital technologies become powerful tools for discovery-based and problem-orientated learning, allowing pupils to construct new understandings and expertise through technology-based exploratory activity.

Collins and Berge (1996) list a number of important changes for learners, among them the need to *construct* knowledge rather than *receive* it, focus on its use, solve problems rather than memorize facts, ask and refine their own questions and search for answers, work independently and autonomously with a wide range of resources, as well as collaboratively with others.

EDUCATIONAL APPLICATIONS WITHIN THE CONTEXT OF FL LEARNING AND TEACHING

The term 'digital technologies' comprises a wide range of concepts and definitions (see e.g. Churchill, 2007). Due to the vast number of digital learning tools available (see e.g. Kapor, 2008), a general typology is needed to help identify applications for specific learning needs. Various tools – especially in the field of FLs teaching and learning – are categorized in rather general terms: there are tools for audio, video, images, mind mapping, etc. In order to support you with finding tools for your lessons from the extensive pool available (see e.g. Stöcklin, 2012), the concept of 'pedagogic applications for classroom use', so-called 'Educational Applications', will be used here.

As noted earlier, the term *app* tends to be associated with mobile devices (e.g. applications for mobile phones, tablets, etc.). However, here the concept of Educational Applications will be used in a more general sense with a particular focus on the pedagogic use of browser-based applications for computers and tablets.

Educational Applications can be analysed against certain pedagogic quality criteria (see also Seipold, Pachler, Bachmair and Doebeli-Honegger, 2013; Iberer *et al.*, 2010; Strasser, 2012a). We advocate the use of pedagogic criteria here as a mechanism for helping you with separating applications with no or only peripheral use for classroom-based teaching and learning from those that clearly have didactic potential. Educational Applications do not represent a 'new' didactic approach, but rather allow you to combine social constructivist perspectives of learning with the use of Web 2.0 tools within the classroom. Our discussion here is not intended to be exhaustive, but instead we hope to encourage you to search for tools yourself and to use them based on the quality criteria set out and to share them with your community (see the concept of the 'networked teacher'; Baker-Doyle, 2011).

THE PEDAGOGIC DOMAIN

This domain of Educational Applications mainly focuses on learning modes and group-dynamics, i.e. on how pupils can self-direct and teachers can foster learning processes. These criteria can be considered to be cultural techniques that enhance learning and support the concept of a (virtual) learning community:

Reflection

Educational Applications that help pupils and teachers reflect or give feedback on a certain working process. By constantly giving feedback on an expected learning outcome, a work-in-progress philosophy supports an improvement of the final product (e.g. writing a wiki text together based on feedback from peers and self-reflection).

Modification

Educational Applications that make it possible for the whole group to produce outcomes and adapt them individually to their own learning needs (e.g. when using a cartoon application, learners can save and adapt their outcome by adding new frames, changing new speech bubbles, etc.).

Communication

Educational Applications that enable learners to communicate about their learning progress within working processes. The advantage here is that learners can use the L2 to discuss work-in-progress (e.g. when using a collaborative text-production tool such as Edupad (http://www.edupad.ch/), they can ask questions their peers can answer).

Multiplication

Educational Applications that allow the sharing of artefacts with colleagues. Highly creative products should be disseminated (e.g. Facebook/Twitter share button, copy links or embed a created quiz into a virtual learning environment).

Creation

Educational Applications that address the learner's productive/creative potential. Pupils and teachers can create learning and teaching materials themselves (e.g. creation of a radio show about a relevant topic).

Collaboration

Educational Applications that enable social-constructivist collaboration (see e.g., Dinevski and Arh, 2012), i.e. the teacher does not act as a knowledge provider, but as a communicative collaborator (see e.g. Strasser, 2011; Heckmann and Strasser, 2012) on a hierarchically de-verticalized level, i.e. all learning peers are equal. The principle of collaboration represents an interesting addendum to the common approach of mono-directional error detection in the FL lesson (i.e. the teacher only acts as the supervisor, who detects and corrects mistakes). Learning outcomes (e.g. the collaborative production of a mind map with Padlet [http://padlet.com]) can be achieved collaboratively without the sole focus on *linguistic infelicities*. Of course, language mistakes should be corrected and improved, but with collaborative Educational Applications this happens through a constructive and supportive discourse, i.e. before a discussion of mistakes takes place, linguistically versatile and well-performed structures are highlighted.

THE DIDACTIC DOMAIN

This domain is mainly dedicated to the *what* of FL teaching with new learning technologies or Educational Applications. Several categories of skills and competences can be acquired in the FL lesson (see e.g. Harmer, 2010; Thaler, 2012). The didactic domain of Educational Applications implies a rather general approach, the focus on the skills of reading, writing, listening, monologic and dialogic speaking (see Council of Europe, 2001). The aim of this domain is mainly to emphasize that the use of Educational Applications does not focus on the support of learners' technological skills but mainly on language learning skills considering also grammatical and lexical aspects. Due to the rise of educational technology in the field of FL learning, many tools have been developed that support various skills. There is a wide range of applications: cartoon tools such as ToonDoo (http://www.toondoo.com/) for writing, podcasting tools such as Audioboo (http://audioboo.fm/) for speaking and listening or various Quiz generators such as Learning Applications (such as http://www.learningapps.org) for reading and testing of cognitive knowledge.

THE PRAGMATIC DOMAIN

Apart from didactic and pedagogic benefits Educational Applications can have in the FL classroom, certain pragmatic difficulties concerning the use of internet tools need to be considered.

Table 11.1 clearly shows that the use of new learning technologies, such as Educational Applications, poses challenges. However, most of the problem solutions outlined do not require superb technical equipment or profound technical expertise, but rather a general didactic talent to re-shape certain blended learning scenarios (i.e. the combination of classroom training and the use of the computer) adapted to the given situation in the classroom.

Table 11.1 Potential problems with the use of digital technologies in FL teaching and learning and possible solutions

Problem	Possible solutions
1 tools are too complex to use	• avoid tools that require profound expert knowledge concerning usability • avoid tools that need to be installed locally
2 tools are not relevant for the FL teaching curriculum (e.g. tools are of no use from a pedagogic perspective, e.g. politically incorrect contents, sites with dubious advertisements, etc.)	• avoid sites and tools that are of doubtful origin • use tools and pages that explicitly cooperate with educational institutions or have serious sources as references (e.g. as seen on CNN, BBC, TechCrunch, etc.)
3 tools that are expensive	• social media and Educational Applications imply free, community-based possibilities to collaboratively generate or adapt knowledge. Browse through various edu-blogging sites (http://larryferlazzo.edublogs.org/), which frequently offer free alternatives to paid ones • Web 2.0-providers often offer premium accounts for money; educators often get these premium accounts for free
4 lack of hardware*	• two or three pupils working with one device • dividing work into computer-based tasks and non computer-based tasks • internet tasks as homework • fund-raising initiatives for self-access room
5 pupils' lack of media literacy	• introductory lessons • practicing skills like skimming, scanning, using search engines • raising awareness of problems, e.g. information overload • evaluating the reliability of websites
6 time-consuming and ineffective surfing	• using WebQuests (http://webquest.org/) or web-units • pre-selecting websites (using social bookmarking tools such as Diigo (http://www.diigo.com/) • setting precise tasks and instructions • setting time limits • providing guidance through worksheets • requiring presentation of results (with sources)
7 conflict between time required and demands by the curriculum	• reduction to 1–2 projects per year • starting with a mini-project • replacement of related textbook unit by internet project
8 problems with e-mail exchanges	• sticking to the 10 Golden Rules by Donath (http://www.englisch.schule.de/email.htm) • using tested and documented projects

Problem	Possible solutions
9 language mistakes in texts	• raising awareness of authenticity • analysis in class to create language awareness • editing and correcting own texts
10 communication tools: uncontrolled interaction	• using closed channels and fora • setting topics and tasks • analysing texts (log files)
11 presentations: form before content	• insisting on the 'content is king' principle: what is said is more important than multimedia gimmicks • making grading transparent (evaluation sheet) • discussing good/bad websites/presentations

* Examples 4–11 are taken from Thaler, 2012, p. 72

EDUCATIONAL APPLICATIONS IN A NUTSHELL

Good Educational Applications try to combine all the benefits and obstacles of the pedagogic, didactic and pragmatic domains, but avoid classroom use of tools that is unethical, overpriced and full of advertisements since these aspects are normally distractors from the actual collaborative learning process. Furthermore, Educational Applications should not be too technologically sophisticated concerning usability. By reducing complex usability and the focus on didactic versatility, the aspect of intrinsic motivation among teachers and learners to use simple but effective tools in the FL classroom can be intensified. Many obstacles concerning the use of digital technologies/Educational Applications are often perceptual. On the whole, an application can be considered to be educational if the majority of working modes (e.g. collaboration, reflection, etc.) can be applied in the pedagogic domain, at least one skill (e.g. writing) is practised in the didactic domain and several obstacles from the pragmatic domain (e.g. inappropriate contents) can be considered redundant.

EDUCATIONAL APPLICATIONS APPLIED

Practical examples

In order to get a more practical view of Educational Applications, the following example is provided[1]:

Application		Tricider (http://www.tricider.com; similar applications are: http://www.proconlists.com and http://www.thinkmeter.com.)
Focus		Exchange ideas/opinions online; formulate phrases expressing your point of view in L2.
Time		60 mins.
ICT-skills		Very basic (browsing, uploading, typing, sharing).
Equipment		Computer lab or private computer, projector, internet access.
Setting		At school or outside school (at home, café, etc.).
Preparation	1	Go to http://www.tricider.com. In case you want to store all your discussions, you can register for free. N.B.: Tricider offers special plans for teachers (premium accounts, etc.).

Application		Tricider (http://www.tricider.com; similar applications are: http://www.proconlists.com and http://www.thinkmeter.com.)
	2	Then formulate a question pupils should discuss. Click 'Go'. In this example, we want to initiate a discussion about 'the pros and cons of life in the city'. Image 1: Starting your discussion
	3	Then click 'add a description' and specify the task. Click 'save', then 'share and invite'. Image 2: Specifying the task
	4	Now you can invite your pupils to participate via mail or just copy the link for classroom use. Image 3: Inviting participants
In class	1	Provide the given URL to your pupils. Depending on the amount of computers available, arrange groups. Ask pupils to find as many arguments as possible for and against 'life in the city' considering the following aspects: • economic aspects (job situation, commuting, rent, shopping, etc.); • private aspects (family, entertainment, etc.); • ecological aspects (public transport, noise, pollution, etc.); N.B. your pupils do not have to register for Tricider.

Application		Tricider (http://www.tricider.com; similar applications are: http://www.proconlists.com and http://www.thinkmeter.com.)
	2	Give your pupils plenty of time to formulate their opinions. They access the URL provided, click 'add idea' and fill out the given fields. In the field with the light bulb the general argument should be formulated, in the field 'add a description' pupils should write longer texts providing argumentation. Emphasise the need for complete sentences and fully formulated ideas. 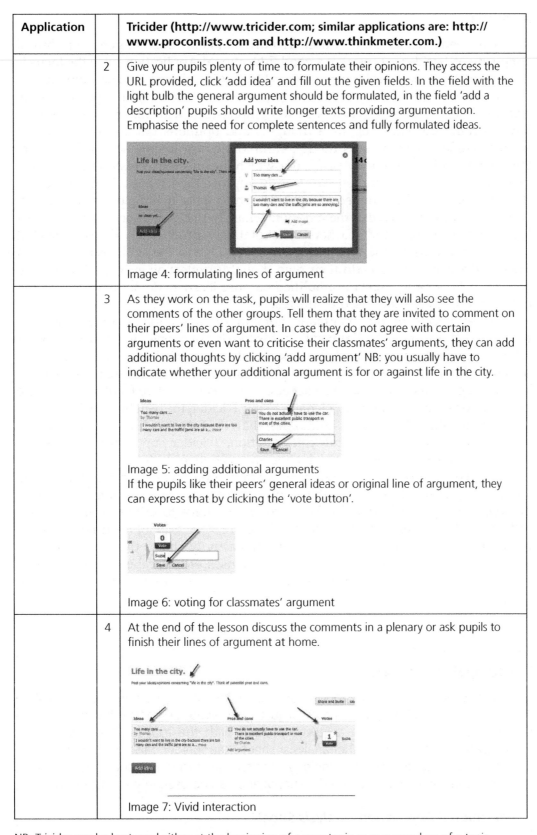 Image 4: formulating lines of argument
	3	As they work on the task, pupils will realize that they will also see the comments of the other groups. Tell them that they are invited to comment on their peers' lines of argument. In case they do not agree with certain arguments or even want to criticise their classmates' arguments, they can add additional thoughts by clicking 'add argument' NB: you usually have to indicate whether your additional argument is for or against life in the city. Image 5: adding additional arguments If the pupils like their peers' general ideas or original line of argument, they can express that by clicking the 'vote button'. Image 6: voting for classmates' argument
	4	At the end of the lesson discuss the comments in a plenary or ask pupils to finish their lines of argument at home. Image 7: Vivid interaction

NB: Tricider can be best used either at the beginning of a new topic or as a round-up of a topic discussed in class before.

NB: Since the nature of the Internet is very transient, tools come and go. However, the focus in this activity is not on the tool or technology itself but rather on the didactic scenario (what you can do with it). Once you understand how 'decision-making tools' such as Tricider work in general and how to embed them in a methodological context, the skills become transferable across tools which is one of the main concepts underpinning Educational Applications.

Analysis

As can be seen, Tricider is a very user-friendly, hands-on tool. The general technical simplicity of Tricider is typical of a good Educational Application since the focus is clearly put on pedagogic/didactic versatility. Taking the pedagogic domain into consideration, various cultural techniques are supported within the context of Tricider. The aspect of *reflection* is clearly emphasized with this tool since pupils have to come up with their own thoughts and opinions but are also explicitly invited to reflect on their peers' thoughts and counterarguments (see e.g. Eydelman, 2011). Learners can constantly *modify* (for which they need to register) their written texts and opinions so that they can steadily improve their written inputs based on the learners' or teacher's remedial input. The third most striking pedagogic aspect is that of *collaboration*. One of the most vital characteristics of a socio-constructivist learning tool, pupils and teachers collaboratively produce an FL-topic related stream of input using the target language (TL). Due to the egalitarian nature of Tricider (i.e. everyone can add their own thoughts, reflect on everyone's opinions, etc.), the collaborative aspect is amplified because learners do not have the feeling of being constantly supervised by the teacher.

Various aspects of the pragmatic domain do not apply with Tricider. As mentioned above, it can be claimed that this tool is not *complex* to use. In case your school is *not really well-equipped*, the task can also be carried out as an assignment outside school. In case of *linguistic infelicities* within the discussion stream of Tricider, the pupils as well as the teacher can give constructive feedback when the pros and cons are discussed in a plenary. Using Tricider, the benefits of collaborative performance should be emphasized rather than the focus on linguistic perfection. Taking the didactic domain into consideration, Tricider supports various skills within a collaborative context: productive and receptive skills are practised. Since pupils have to provide topic-relevant written input whilst at the same time considering linguistic accuracy, the skill of writing can be considered vital with Tricider (see e.g. Pop, 2011). Furthermore, pupils have to critically analyse and reflect on their peers' written input. Therefore, the skill of reading plays an important role with Tricider. In addition, this activity shows that pupils need to consider grammar (word order, use of correct tenses, etc.), vocabulary (use of topic-related words/phrases) and discursive strategies (e.g. coherently replying to one of their peers' statements).

Task 11.1

EDU-application check

Pick a Web 2.0 tool of your choice or take an application from http://cooltoolsforschools.wikispaces.com or just type 'Web 2.0 tools education' into your search engine. Try to acquaint yourself with the tool (usability, didactic application), then fill in the analysis sheet (see below; also online: http://telelearning-reloaded.com/technology_chapter) in order to find out if the application can be considered educational and can be used in your classroom.[2]

Educational Application Analysis Sheet[3]

tool:	link:
last access on:	category (audio, video, etc.)

Pedagogic domain

	tool supports	examples
collaboration	O	
communication	O	
multiplication	O	
creation	O	
reflection	O	
modification	O	
total	…../6	minimum of three ticks
This application can be considered …	O educational O non-educational[4]	in the pedagogic domain

Didactic domain

	tool supports	examples
writing	O	
reading	O	
listening	O	
monologic speaking	O	
dialogic speaking	O	
total	…../5	minimum of two ticks
This application can be considered …	O educational O non-educational	in the didactic domain

Pragmatic domain[5]

problem	possible solution	check
tools are too complex to use	• avoid tools that require profound expert knowledge concerning usability • avoid tools that need to be installed locally	O
tools are not relevant for the FL teaching curriculum (e.g. tools are of no use from a pedagogic perspective, e.g. politically incorrect contents, sites with dubious advertisements, etc.)	• avoid sites and tools that are of doubtful origin • use tools and pages that explicitly cooperate with educational institutions or have serious sources as references (e.g. as seen on CNN, BBC, TechCrunch, etc.)	O

tools that are expense	• social media and Educational Applications imply free, community-based possibilities to collaboratively generate or adapt knowledge; Browse through various edu-blogging sites (http://larryferlazzo. edublogs.org/), which frequently offer free alternatives to paid ones. • Web 2.0-providers often offer premium accounts for money; Educators often get these premium accounts for free	O
		O
		O
This application can be considered …	O educational O non-educational	in the pragmatic domain

Summary

Pedagogic domain	O educational	O non-educational
Didactic domain	O educational	O non-educational
Pragmatic domain	O educational	O non-educational
Total:	O educational	O non-educational
Didactic scenario	positive features	negative features

Task 11.2

Analyse difficulties

Think of a tool that you have recently used in class that caused various difficulties. Analyse the didactic scenario filling in the Educational Application Analysis Sheet. What's your score? What were the main obstacles? Do the problem solution proposals in the pragmatic domain give you some insights of how to avoid certain obstacles?

Task 11.3

Share the good work

Join a Facebook group such as EUROCALL, the IATEFL LT SIG or a Twitter hashtag community like #tefl #edchat to post your positive experience with a certain Educational Application. Mention your main insights considering the Educational Application Analysis Sheet.

CONCLUSION

The use of digital technologies in the FL lesson has become quite prominent within the last few years. One of the reasons why the use of the internet plays a considerable role in the classroom is that certain tools (e.g. Educational Applications) are becoming more and more user-friendly and less complex: 'Technology is increasingly ubiquitous in the world around us, and if used in a principled manner, can support and enhance … language learning.' (Hockly, 2011. p. 111). We would place the emphasis on the word *support*. Educational technologists and FL teachers tend to agree on the fact that the computer *per se* will not replace the teacher, but that digital tools when used in a principled manner can improve certain socio-constructivist learning processes, especially in times where instructional classroom training is still predominant (see e.g. Bauer, 2012). Therefore, digital technologies such as Educational Apps, combine basic teaching and learning principles from the analogue classroom settings and transfer these into the digital context. Educational Apps are not supposed to be a revolutionary approach to FL learning and teaching but can offer an interesting, motivational alternative meeting the zeitgeist of young learners (see e.g. Brandhofer, 2012). The combination of the pedagogic, pragmatic and didactic domain with Educational Applications can help ensure that language teachers and learners use various tools within a blended learning context that do not exclusively focus on complex technological procedures, but more on the pedagogic and didactic aspects of language teaching and learning.

NOTES

1   For more practical examples, see Strasser 2012b.

2   For an Educational Application Analysis Sheet sample, see: http://learning-reloaded.com/technology_chapter

3   For a theoretical and practical background, see Pachler, Evans, Redondo and Fisher, 2014.

4   The dichotomy educational/non-educational is indicative and intended as a reference point only.

5   Only the most common obstacles are listed here.

REFERENCES

Bachmair, B. and Pachler, N. (2013) 'Composition and appropriation in a culture characterised by provisionality', in Böck, M. and Pachler, N. (eds) *Multimodality and Social Semiosis: Communication, Meaning-Making and Learning in the Work of Gunther Kress.* New York: Routledge, pp. 211–220.

Baker-Doyle, K. (2011) *The Networked Teacher. How New Teachers Build Social Networks for Professional Support.* New York & London: Teachers College Press Columbia University.

Bauer, R. (2012) 'We Are Not A Gadget'. Warum die Schule auch in Zukunft Lehrerinnen und Lehrer noch braucht', in Blaschitz E., Brandhofer, G. Nosko, C. and Schwed G. (eds) *Zukunft des Lernens. Wie digitale Medien Schule, Aus- und Weiterbildung verändern.* Glückstadt: Verlag Werner Hülsbusch, pp. 111–126.

Brandhofer, G. (2012) 'Die Didaktik der Zukunft. Fabelhafter Unterricht jenseits neurodidaktischer Moden', in Blaschitz E., Brandhofer, G. Nosko, C. and Schwed G. (eds) *Zukunft des Lernens. Wie digitale Medien Schule, Aus- und Weiterbildung verändern.* Glückstadt: Verlag Werner Hülsbusch, pp. 127–144.

Buchberger, G., Chardaloupa, J., Perperidis, G. and Heckmann, V. (2011) 'Fremdsprachen. Mit Technologien Sprachen lernen und lehren', in Ebner, M. and Schön, S. (eds) *L3T. Lehrbuch für Lernen und Lehren mit Technologien*. 1st edition. Berlin; Heidelberg: epubli.de, pp. 435–442.

Chang, S. (2004) 'The roles of mentors in electronic learning environments'. *AACE Journal* 12(3), pp. 331–342.

Churchill, D. (2007) 'Web 2.0 and possibilities for educational applications'. *Educational Technology Publications: Educational Technology*, 47(2), pp. 24–29.

Cole, J. and Foster, H. (2008) *Using Moodle*. 2nd edition. Beijing, Cambridge, Farnham, Köln, Paris, Sebastopol, Taipei, Tokyo: O'Reilly.

Collins, M. and Berge, Z. (1996) 'Facilitating interaction in computer mediated online courses'. Background information paper for a presentation at the FSU/AECT Distance Education Conference, Tallahassee, Fl. 1996. Available online at: http://repository.maestra.net/valutazione/MaterialeSarti/articoli/Facilitating%20Interaction.htm

Council of Europe (2001) *Common European Framework of References for Languages. Learning, Teaching, Assessment*. Cambridge: Cambridge University Press.

Dinevski, D. and Arh, T. (2012) 'Web 2.0 technologies for e-learning', in Etxeberria, A.L. (ed.) *Global e-learning*. Madrid: Ediciones CEF, pp. 175–184.

Eydelman, N. (2011) 'A way with wikis in the EFL writing classroom', in Pattison, T. (ed.) *IATEFL 2011. Brighton Conference Selections*. 45th International Conference Brighton 15–19 April 2011, pp. 115–116.

Harmer, J. (2010) *The Practice of English Language Teaching*. 4th edition. Harlow: Pearson Longman.

Heckmann, V. and Strasser, T. (2012) 'Von der technischen Komplexität hin zur didaktischen Vielseitigkeit – "3-Clicks-Edu-Apps" zur Steigerung der Sprechkompetenz im fremdsprachlichen Unterricht', in Kapp-Kawermann, M. (ed.) *Zeitschrift für e-learning, Lernkultur und Bildungstechnologie* 2 2012, pp. 34–36.

Hockly, N. 'Tweeting is for the birds – not for language learning (2011)'. ELT Journal/ IATEFL Debate, in Pattison, T. (ed.) *IATEFL 2011. Brighton Conference Selections*. 45th International Conference Brighton 15–19 April 2011, pp. 110–112.

Iberer, U., Simon, F. and Spannagel, C. (2010) 'Bildungsmanagement 2.0. Potenziale und Anforderungen von Social Software in Bildungsorganisationen', in Schweizer, G., Müller, U. and Adam, T. (eds) *Wert und Werte im Bildungsmanagement. Nachhaltigkeit – Ethik – Bildungscontrolling*. Bielefeld: W. Bertelsmann, pp. 241–257.

Kapor, M. (2008) 'Information hydrant'. A FlickR image. FlickR. Available online at: http://www.flickr.com/photos/will-lion/2595497078/

Kress, G. and Pachler, N. (2007) 'Thinking about the 'm-' in mobile learning', in Pachler, N. (2007) (ed.) *Mobile learning: towards a research agenda*. London: WLE Centre Occasional Papers in Work-based Learning 1, pp. 7–32. Available at: http://www.wlecentre.ac.uk/cms/files/occasionalpapers/mobilelearning_pachler_2007.pdf

Pachler, N., Evans, M., Redondo, A. and Fisher, L. (2014) *Learning to Teach Foreign Languages in the Secondary School. A Companion to School Experience*. 4th edition. London; New York: Routledge.

Pop, A. (2011) 'Integrating asynchronous writing and speaking tools for EFL learning optimisation', in Pattison, T. (ed.) *IATEFL 2011. Brighton Conference Selections*. 45th International Conference Brighton 15–19 April 2011, pp. 113–114.

Schiefner, M. and Kerres, M. (2011) 'Web 2.0 in der Hochschullehre', in Dittler, U. (ed.) *E-Learning: Einsatzkonzepte und Erfolgsfaktoren des Lernens it interaktiven Medien*. München: Odenbourg.

Seipold, J., Pachler, N., Bachmair, B. and Doebeli-Honegger, B. (2013) 'Mobile learning: strategies for planning and implementing learning with mobile devices in secondary school contexts', in Leask, M. and Pachler, N. (eds) *Learning to Teach using ICT in the Secondary School*. 3rd edition. London: Routledge, pp. 185–204.

Stöcklin, N. (2012) 'Von analog zu digital: die neuen Herausforderungen für die Schule', in Blaschitz, E., Brandhofer, G., Nosko, C. and Schwed, G. (eds) *Zukunft des Lernens. Wie digitale Medien Schule, Aus- und Weiterbildung verändern*. Glückstadt: Verlag Werner Hülsbusch, pp. 57–74.

Strasser, T. (2011) 'Moodle im Fremdsprachenunterricht. Blended Learning als innovativer didaktischer Ansatz oder pädagogische Eintagsfliege'. Glückstadt: Verlag Werner: Hülsbusch.

Strasser, T. (2012a) 'A change of paradigm with Web 2.0? Why educational applications might be worth a try', in Etxeberria, A.L. (ed.) *Global e-learning*. Madrid: Ediciones CEF, pp. 135–144.

Strasser, T. (2012b) *Mind the App! Inspiring Internet Tools and Activities to Engage your Students*. Rum/Innsbruck: Helbling Languages.

Thaler, E. (2012) *Englisch unterrichten. Grundlagen, Kompetenzen, Methoden*. Berlin, Heidelberg: Cornelsen.

Wiley, D. and Hilton, J. (2009) 'Openness, Dynamic Specialization, and the Disaggregated Future of Higher Education'. *International Review of Researchin Open and Distance Learning*, 10(5), pp. 1–15. Available online at: http://www.irrodl.org/index.php/irrodl/article/view/768/1415

USEFUL LINKS

http://fremdsprachenundneuemedien.blogspot.com/
Jürgen Wagner's blog and links on teaching English with new media

http://www.freetech4teachers.com/
Free Technology for Teachers by Richard Byrne

http://nikpeachey.blogspot.com/
Nik's Learning Technology Blog
Nik Peachey
For English Language Teachers
Chapter 12 Links

http://edtechtoolbox.blogspot.com
EdTech Toolbox
A place to share e-learning and Web 2.0 tools for education. Computers and laptops in education are important only when used with good pedagogy. Digital content and creation is an important part of the process for educators in the 21st century.

http://usingictinfe.blogspot.com/
Using ICT in Further Education
Free Resources for teachers and students (Open Source, Freeware, Creative Commons)
Patricia Donaghy

http://lifefeast.blogspot.com/
Ana María Menzes blogging on New Media

http://quickshout.blogspot.com/
Nik's QuickShout
Educational Technology and ELT

http://coolcatteacher.blogspot.com/
Cool Cat Teacher Blog
Teaching students with new tools, enthusiasm, and belief that teaching is a noble calling
Vicki Davis

http://www.markbrumley.com/
Mark Brumley: Educational Technology

http://ozgekaraoglu.edublogs.org/
  Ozge Karaoglu's Blog
  About teaching, learning, reflecting and being a 21st century learner and teacher

http://teachertrainingvideos.com/
  TeacherTraining Videos by Russell Stannard

http://www.commoncraft.com/
  The CommonCraft Show by Lee LeFever

http://theedublogger.com/
  The Edublogger: Tips and Tricks for Educators

http://cyber-kap.blogspot.com/
  Technology Tidbits: Thoughts of a Cyber Hero
  David Kapuler

http://www.mguhlin.org/
  Around the Corner-MGuhlin.org

http://www.ictineducation.org/
  ICT in Education
  The Educational Technology Site

http://techtipsforteachersblog.blogspot.com/
  Tech Tips for Teachers

http://www.learning-reloaded.com
  Learning with New Technologies
  Thomas Strasser

http://www.livebinders.com/play/play_or_edit?id=26329
  Web 2.0 tools
  Suzie Vesper

http://cooltoolsforschools.wikispaces.com/
  Web 2.0 tools collection

http://technology4kids.pbworks.com/w/page/24292734/FrontPage
  Great collection using new technologies with kids
  Shelly S. Terrell

http://www.scoop.it/t/web-2-0-tools-for-language-learning
  Web 2.0 for language learning
  Vicky Saumell

http://www.classroom20.com/
  Web 2.0 in the classroom
  Steve Hargadon

http://edtech-hub.blogspot.co.at/
  Tools for teaching with technology

http://larryferlazzo.edublogs.org/2010/06/28/my-best-posts-for-tech-novices-plus-one-
  from-somebody-else/
  Posts for tech novices
  Larry Ferlazzo

A SELECTION OF EDUCATIONAL APPLICATIONS*

tool	link	similar application	pedagogic domain	didactic domain	use in the FL lesson
Learning Apps (Quiz generator)	www.learningapps.org	www.quizlet.com	collaboration, multiplication, modification, creation	reading, listening, writing	• grammar/vocabulary check-up • practicing listening/writing skills
Wordle (tag clouds)	www.wordle.net	www.tagxedo.com	reflection, modification, communication, collaboration	reading, writing, speaking	• text interpretation (songs, speeches, poems, etc.) • lexical work (learning vocab) • cultural studies
Glogster (interactive learning environments)	www.glogster.com		reflection, modification, creation, communication, collaboration	reading, writing, listening	• learners create personal profile (introducing myself) • learners/teachers create a surface for a special topic • book report • profile of a famous person • collect quotations and analyse them
ScreenR (video casting application)	www.screenr.com	http://screencastle.com	reflection, modification, communication, multiplication, creation, collaboration	reading, listening, writing, speaking	• analysis of a website in the FL • producing tutorials using L2 • giving feedback on written assignments
PiratePad (collaborative text writing surface)	www.piratepad.net	www.edupad.ch	reflection, modification, communication, multiplication, creation, collaboration	reading, writing	• writing various text types together (fairy tales, adventure stories, etc.) • brainstorming in L2 • learners give feedback on teacher's lesson in L2

* Depending on the actual use of a certain tool in the FL lesson, the pedagogic and didactic domain may vary. The chart serves as a framework or orientation to help you with how certain tools can be used in the FL lesson. We are aware of the fact that various tools can be used in different ways (e.g. in ways not listed in this chart).

continued

Voicethread (multi-media brainstorming)	www.voicethread.com	reflection, modification, communication, multiplication, creation, collaboration	reading, writing, listening, speaking	• brainstorming on a certain topic in L2 • research map (collecting information on a certain topic in L2) • radio show (podcast) • picture description • comparisons • fluency competition (learners have to talk about a certain picture as fluently as possible)
Padlet (digital mind mapping tool)	www.padlet.com	reflection, communication, creation, collaboration, multiplication	reading, writing, listening	• brainstorming on a certain topic in L2 • giving feedback in L2 • who-am-I-quiz (teacher posts hints about a celebrity day by day, learners have to guess who it is) • a word a day: teacher posts a new word, idiom, etc. every day; pupils try to find a translation and write a contextualized sentence
Audioboo (podcasting application)	www.audioboo.fm	reflection, modification, creation, communication, collaboration	listening, speaking, writing, reading	• teacher speaks assignment • create a radio show • pupils record their opinion on a controversial topic in L2 • pupils read certain texts (poems, novels, etc.) and record themselves • book report – the spoken way: pupils create a book report via Audioboo
Toondoo (cartoon application)	www.toondoo.com	creation, modification, collaboration	reading, writing	• pupils create cartoons about a certain topic in the FLs classroom • teacher creates cartoons with certain target vocabulary in L2
Cueprompter	www.cueprompter.com	creation, modification, collaboration	writing, reading, speaking	• pupils write a news announcement in L2 • pupils perform a presidential speech in L2 • casting show: students read a news announcement as part of the news anchorman/woman casting

1 *Examples 4–11 are taken from Thaler, 2012, p. 72*

Chapter 12 Primary Foreign Languages and Key Stage 2–3 transfer

NALINI BOODHOO

BY THE END OF THIS CHAPTER YOU SHOULD:

- have developed understanding of the primary languages context;
- have considered the issues surrounding the successful teaching and learning of primary languages;
- have considered some good practice ideas appropriate for teaching primary languages;
- have an appreciation of the issues related to transition and transfer issues in order to ensure continued progress for KS2 pupils with prior experience of learning a foreign language (FL).

THE CONTEXT OF PRIMARY FLS

The learning of FLs is an entitlement for primary school children. This chapter aims to provide secondary language student teachers with information and guidance which will help develop the skills, understanding and knowledge to collaborate with primary school teachers and ensure children make continued progress in their FL learning in secondary school.

Throughout the last decade and more there has been considerable debate about the provision of FLs in English primary schools. Building on a policy initially elaborated by the Labour Government, provision in Key Stage 2 (i.e. from Year 3 to Year 6) is due to become statutory in 2014. The commitment to make this a reality has been embodied in an entitlement for primary schools children in England to learn at least one FL in this age phase (see http://www.education.gov.uk/schools/teachingandlearning/ curriculum/nationalcurriculum2014/nationalcurriculum and http://www.education. gov.uk/schools/teachingandlearning/curriculum/nationalcurriculum2014/).

This decision will hopefully be a further step towards realising the continuity, synergy and lifelong learning promoted in the *Nuffield Languages Inquiry* published over a decade ago (The Nuffield Foundation, 2000). This publication considered the UK's 'capability in languages' as the authors were tasked 'to report on what we need to do as a nation to improve it ' (p. 4). In 2002 the *National Languages Strategy* (DfES, 2002) was published setting out a vision of lifelong language learning commencing with early years provision focused on an entitlement for children to develop an interest in the culture of other nations. The study of at least one of the working languages of the European Union was envisaged to be delivered (in full or in part) in class time. Formal recognition of achievement was anticipated through the *Common European Framework* by the age of 11. Other more recent reviews of policy such as *The Languages Review: Final Report* (Dearing and King, 2007) and the *Independent Review of the Primary Curriculum: Final Report* (Rose, 2009) have also supported the case for the teaching of primary FLs.

As a result of the shifts in policy the now defunct Centre for Information on Language Teaching and Research/National Centre for Languages (CILT), which developed projects across England and Wales, and the also now defunct National Advisory Centre for Early Language Learning (NACELL) were established to develop the provision of early language learning, offering a wealth of guidance. NACELL merged with the Primary Languages Training Zone to create one 'national gateway', which continues to provide support, advice and information for teachers and others (see http://www.primarylanguages.org.uk) through a web archive.

Whilst at the time of writing, provision is not yet uniform across England in meeting the entitlement to learn a FL, one key finding from a survey carried out by the National Foundation for Educational Research (2009) shows that 92% of schools were offering FLs in class time with French featuring as the most common language offered followed by Spanish and German. The survey also revealed that:

> the proportion of schools where there were staff with training but no qualifications, or neither training nor qualifications, was quite high, but so was the proportion of schools where staff had a language degree. In fact, there were 13 per cent of schools reporting that all their staff teaching languages had a language degree.
>
> (Wade *et al.*, 2009, p. 7)

The most common model for teaching primary languages, according to the survey, was discrete lessons with schools providing one lesson a week. Programmes tended to be based upon the non-statutory *KS2 Framework for Languages* (since withdrawn by the Coalition government, but at the time of writing still available on the National Archive; DfES/QCA, 2007) with the use of commercial Schemes of Work proliferating, as well as those produced by the schools and Local Authorities.

Whilst the above seems to paint a positive picture in the growth of the provision of languages in primary schools, variability is a key characteristic. The factors contributing to this relate to issues such as lack of appropriate materials in schools, the number of trained primary FLs teachers and continued professional development for those without a good grasp of L2. For a more detailed outline of the challenges see Jones and McLachlan (2009, pp. 12–15).

Against this background it is to be noted that the introduction of FLs into the primary curriculum is not without controversy. The evidence base for establishing a place of FL learning in the primary curriculum is mixed, given many of the studies carried out make it difficult to compare 'like with like' – these have been carried out in different countries where cultural contexts are different, as are the educational purposes proposed to promote FLs and the approach adopted to teaching and learning. Whilst the 'critical period hypothesis theory' suggests it is better to start young as children can acquire L2 in a similar vein to their mother tongue, questions do arise in this debate relating to what the benefits of learning a FL might be both generally and for early starters, whether these benefits might be only linguistic or encompass a wider sphere, including the affective domains, personal and social learning, cultural understanding and precisely what the optimum age might be to start learning a FL. Some studies indicate the 'older the faster' – that is, older children acquire FLs at a faster rate as their cognitive resources are more developed (Muñoz, 2006). There is also a wide literature which focuses on advantages of learning through the medium of more than the mother tongue (as in the case of bilingual education) and the links between cognitive and linguistic development. One study about elementary students in the US, cited in an international review of primary languages, found that 'the longer pupils study a foreign language, the higher their level of achievement in standardised tests in maths and English' (Caccavale, 2007) and development in critical thinking/problem solving skills. Demonstrating the complexity of apparent gains, the author suggests that where literacy gains are evident this might be due to increased cognitive ability and not just skills transferred from FL learning.

It is important, therefore, to be clear about why FLs should have a place in the primary curriculum and more practical questions such as how to ensure proficiency gains if children are expected to make them. The conditions, which appear to favour success in language learning in the primary school, relate to a rich syllabus content, community support and

> active support from the Head Teacher and the whole staff; clear linguistic and communicative aims; emphasis on enjoyment and enthusiasm; links with foreign countries; knowledge about the culture; e-mail or video-conferencing links; active teaching methods with extensive use of songs and games; ICT, for example, the use of PowerPoint and an interactive whiteboard, integrated into the teaching; sharing of resources and collaborative work with the local MFL secondary department; reliable transfer records; extensive training and support; and links with literacy.
>
> (Hunt *et al.*, 2005: 18)

Task 12.1

Policy and practice

What are the current arguments that drive the continued push for a place for FLs in the primary curriculum? What educational arguments would *you* put forward for the compulsory place for FLs in the primary curriculum? Which *learning theories* and *language learning theories* underpin your views?

To what extent are your arguments supported by the approach adopted by the Key Stage 2 Framework and the National Curriculum guidelines?

KS2 Framework
http://www.primarylanguages.org.uk/policy_and_research/policy_and_reform/key_stage_2_framework.aspx

KS2 Languages Consultation Report
http://www.education.gov.uk/schools/teachingandlearning/curriculum/nationalcurriculum2014/a00221243/ks2-languages-consultation-report

QCDA The National Curriculum Primary Handbook
https://orderline.education.gov.uk/gempdf/184962383X.PDF

DfE National Curriculum
http://www.education.gov.uk/schools/teachingandlearning/curriculum/nationalcurriculum2014

What are the issues that have to be considered at the national, regional and local levels in sustaining FLs in primary schools? What are your personal views about this as a *secondary* school FLs teacher? What are the *local* issues relevant to the introduction/embedding of FLs in the primary curriculum? How widespread is provision?

TEACHER KNOWLEDGE

Underlying issues of progression in language learning is the need to understand how younger children learn languages and to have in place expert teachers who can provide quality teaching. Pupils' growth as learners depends on the competences or 'knowledge, skills and ability of the teacher' (Driscoll *et al.*, 2004: 3). Jones and McLachlan (2009) note that good teaching (and therefore learning of FLs at primary level) depends on teachers having knowledge and understanding of the *principles* underpinning the primary curriculum. Sometimes expert primary teachers lack subject knowledge – principally proficiency in the language(s) being taught and cultural knowledge. It is important to note that subject knowledge for OFSTED (2008, p. 30) includes: knowing how to use the TL with pupils; knowledge and understanding of links with English and literacy, links with other languages (including pupils' own languages); cross-curricular linking; intercultural awareness; statutory and non-statutory guidance for languages; the international dimension and (global) citizenship.

COLLABORATION BETWEEN PRIMARY AND SECONDARY TEACHERS

Secondary language specialists are increasingly requested to carry out cross-phase work with primary class teachers and pupils. There are a number of models which have been developed for working 'collaboratively' such as a lead Languages College working with a cluster of primary schools or Local Authorities coordinating specialist teachers to develop expertise in primary schools. However, effective collaboration depends on a number of factors including mutual understanding and knowledge in both settings about the curriculum and pedagogical approaches. For example, the secondary specialist working in Key Stage 2 needs to develop an appreciation that materials must be matched to the age and linguistic competence of primary pupils. One of the keys to successful cross-phase collaboration is for both primary and secondary specialists to redefine their expertise through learning from and with each other.

Practical steps for student teachers to take

Guidance provided in the Key Stage 2 Framework for Languages (DfES, 2005) is helpful in developing knowledge about Key Stage 2 FLs provision. This document sets out an expectation for the skills pupils should develop by the end of Key Stage 2. It is set out in three parts and focuses on three core strands: Oracy, Literacy and Intercultural Understanding plus two cross-cutting strands: Knowledge about Language (KAL) and Language Learning Strategies (LLS). The document positioned FL learning as an integral part of the primary curriculum and latter sections included information and advice for secondary school teachers. This, taken with the guidance produced in 2009 by the DCSF in *Developing Language in the Primary School: literacy and primary languages,* also situated primary languages in the wider Literacy Strategy for schools. Consequently, teachers perceived the need to exploit and align the links between English and FLs being taught. The Framework was also closely aligned to *Excellence and Enjoyment* (DFES, 2003), which advocated a holistic approach to the primary curriculum through cross-curricular links.

In addition, there existed two sets of Key Stage 2 Schemes of Work which were developed to support language learners to meet the objectives of the Key Stage 2 Framework for Languages. One was published by the Qualifications and Curriculum Authority (DfES/QCA 2007; http://www.primarylanguages.org.uk/resources/schemes_of_work/qcda_schemes_of_work.aspx) and the other by the

TDA (http://www.primarylanguages.org.uk/resources/schemes_of_work/tda_schemes_of_work.aspx). The schemes, available for French, German and Spanish, were optional and could be used in a flexible manner to enhance early language learning and teaching provision.

Task 12.2

Understanding and developing knowledge about the primary languages teaching and learning

What do secondary school teachers need to consider if they are involved in teaching FLs in primary schools? From where would you seek guidance and support?

Analyse some Key Stage 2 Schemes of Work and compare these with what is taught in Year 7. Is there a possible pathway for pupil progression?

Observe some FL lessons in a primary school. Which features of the lesson are similar to secondary schools and which different?

Adapting good practice for KS2

There are many techniques which secondary school teachers can adapt in Key Stage 2 to develop pupils' skills in listening, speaking, reading and writing. It is important for pupils to become autonomous through developing language learning skills which can be beneficial when learning other FLs.

Task 12.3

Adapting existing knowledge, skills and understanding 1

Make a list of teaching and learning aspects of Key Stage 3 practice which are adaptable for Key Stage 2. Complete your list before comparing it with the suggestions below.

Suggestions:

- think about how children learn from visuals (flashcards of objects, word flashcards for developing literacy and associated games/activities such as hide and guess, quick flash, slow reveal, hunt the flashcard memory games, what's missing, keyhole techniques, mini flashcard games such as 'snap'/bingo/dominoes);
- ICT as a medium for learning – IWB activities, website for young learners;
- real and authentic materials (objects to touch and handle, e.g. teach food, drink, clothes, develop all skills areas using menus);
- repetition of vocabulary/phrases/mime/gestures to present and practise language;
- kinaesthetic activities – sentence building with word cards/miming/action and word association;
- group/pair and individual work.

> **Task 12.4**
>
> **Adapting existing knowledge, skills and understanding 2**
>
> Consider the range of activities which primary pupils experience and list those which could be used to teach FLs. Compose your list before looking at the suggestions below.
> Suggestions:
>
> - use of puppets/toys/paper plate masks for role plays;
> - displays – washing line with clothes pegs to display vocabulary/numbers/letters/alphabet frieze, weather boards, clocks, mobiles with classroom phrases/commands;
> - active leaning – singing, clapping or stamping to the rhythm of words and phrases or poems (see Young Pathfinder 6 for ideas);
> - games and materials used for literacy and numeracy in English which can be adapted for the FL;
> - develop intercultural understanding through links with schools abroad as part of an internalisation project (see the British Council website at http://www.britishcouncil.org/etwinning.htm and also http://www.primarylanguages.org.uk/teaching_and_learning/the_international_dimension.aspx), email, video conferencing, visits and development of cross curricular links (geography/history/science);
> - see http://www.primarylanguages.org.uk/teaching_and_learning/active_learning.aspx for more ideas about using rhymes, puppets songs, drama, games storytelling.

KEY STAGE 2–3 PROGRESSION AND TRANSITION

Some studies (Wade *et al.*, 2009 and Evans and Fisher, 2009) have shown that effective transfer of information from primary to secondary schools is an area to be addressed along with more concerted effort to build on pupils' prior learning. Motivation can easily be undermined and the gains of early language learning lost if secondary schools do not build on pupils' prior achievements. Consideration of transfer data and liaison with feeder schools are therefore crucial in order to plan for progression, and increasingly a reappraisal of the teaching materials secondary schools use to ensure flexible planning rather than a curriculum constrained by a particular text book is becoming necessary.

Recently, Evans and Fisher (2012, pp. 165–166) have noted in their study of new emerging communities of practice between primary and secondary schools:

> Where knowledge about prior language learning was acknowledged as important this was usually strategically related to the issue of continuity of learning. Some case study heads of department defined continuity in terms of providing the learners with familiarity in their learning so as to minimise the cultural 'shock' in the school transition…

Variability of FL provision in primary schools is one factor which makes it challenging for secondary school teachers to build effectively upon children's prior learning and skill development given children will arrive from a number of feeder schools. Variability might also encompass children having received different time allocation for the study of languages, differences in teacher quality and a liberal approach to which language is taught whereby children then arrive in secondary schools having learnt different languages to that which is taught in Year 7. Primary school children experience a creative approach to learning across the whole curriculum which generally embraces cross-curricular approaches – a dimension which is not so widespread in secondary schools. Where secondary and primary feeder schools work together in clusters to ensure cross-phase planning greater potential to ensure continued achievement exists. Evans and Fisher (2012) highlight that there are encouraging signs that secondary schools are 'more willing to transform their own provision of foreign language teaching accordingly' (p. 170).

Where collaboration is not possible, portfolios of prior language learning information would enhance transition and enable secondary teachers to understand the skills with which new cohorts arrive. Secondary teachers should be aware of various schemes and portfolios and assessment tools which include the following:

The Junior European Languages Portfolio (ELP)

(http://www.primarylanguages.org.uk/resources/assessment_and_recording/european_languages_portfolio.aspx)

The ELP has been revised to reflect the areas of the Key Stage 2 Framework and includes a language passport (overview of knowledge, experiences of different languages and cultural experiences), a language biography (personalised learning diary) and a dossier (illustrations of achievements). The motivational 'can do' approach allows pupils to record achievement in listening, speaking, reading and writing skill areas. For the document to be useful to secondary teachers it would be helpful for them to know it has been completed through interaction with the teacher and not only by the pupil. It would also be best accompanied by documents which outline actual language skills and language learning skills which have been covered and an assessment of pupils' achievements.

The Languages Ladder

The National Languages Strategy set out in 2002 that 'by age 11 (pupils) should have the opportunity to reach a recognised level of competence on the Common European Framework and for that achievement to be recognised through a national scheme' (p. 15). In 2005, in order to fulfil the objective, the Languages Ladder was designed 'to facilitate formative assessment and to provide short-term motivational goals for learners' (Cable *et al.*, 2010). It is still available in the National Archive (http://webarchive.nationalarchives.gov.uk/20130401151715/https://www.education.gov.uk/publications/eOrderingDownload/20802%20poster%201-4.pdf) and incorporated a 'can do' approach corresponding to the Common European Framework levels.

Asset Languages

Asset languages is the assessment scheme of the OCR Awarding Body (http://www.ocr.org.uk/qualifications/by-type/asset-languages/) designed to reward language learners of all ages and abilities.

Task 12.5

Moving towards smooth transition and progression

Consider what secondary school teachers need to know to ensure a smooth transition for pupils moving up to secondary schools and *why* you need to know about this.

How can you discover what pupils have learned? What do you need to know? (topics/vocabulary/skills developed, assessment practices, pupils attainment and records, period of learning the language – time per week and which year group, which language, language awareness lessons, primary teacher competence).

What conclusions can you draw from this about continuity and progression across key stages?

How can secondary language teachers best make use of induction days for year 6 pupils to value pupils' prior learning? What activities might demonstrate to pupils this prior learning is being valued and thereby ensure continued motivation?

Having considered the above, analyse to what extent the advice and guidance in the KS2 Framework is helpful in addressing issues for successful transition and transfer (See Section 6 of http://www.primarylanguages.org.uk/policy__research/policy_and_reform/idoc.ashx?docid=cb3c0562-6f47-477a-a677-381e3ce7fe31&version=-1).

SUMMARY

Most language teachers and others recognise the huge benefits for primary pupils learning FLs. A focus on language and intercultural learning has the potential to contribute to pupils' development in a way which interconnects with other subject areas. With continued support and teaching of primary languages, plus careful attention to issues of transition which ensure progression across all key stages, it is likely there will be commensurate growth in take up, achievement and attainment in Key Stage 4 and at post-16. The challenge for secondary school teachers is to take account of pupils' prior learning in Key Stage 2 and to build on this so that young learners are motivated and inspired to continue with their FL learning experience. This will necessitate close liaison with primary school colleagues.

REFERENCES

Cable, C. *et al.* (2010) *Languages Learning at Key Stage 2. A longitudinal study, final report.* Open University. DCSF Research Report RR198, London: DCSF.

Caccavale, T. (2007) 'The correlation between early second language learning and native language skill development'. *Learning Languages* 13(1), 31–32.

Dearing, R. and King, L. (2007) *The Languages Review: Final Report.* London: DCSF.

DCSF (2009) *Developing Languages in the Primary School: Literacy and Primary Languages.* London: DCSF.

DfES/QCA (Department for Education and Skills/Qualifications and Curriculum Authority) (2007) *KS2 Schemes of Work.*
French
http://webarchive.nationalarchives.gov.uk/20100612050234/http://www.standards.dfes.gov.uk/schemes3/subjects/primary_mff/?view=get
German
http://webarchive.nationalarchives.gov.uk/20100612050234/http://www.standards.dfes.gov.uk/schemes3/subjects/primary_mfg_new/?view=get

Spanish
http://webarchive.nationalarchives.gov.uk/20100612050234/http://www.standards.dfes.gov.uk/schemes3/subjects/primary_mfs_new/?view=get

DfES (2002) *Languages for All: Languages for Life. A Strategy for England.* London: DfES Publications.

DfES (2003) *Excellence and Enjoyment: A Strategy for primary schools.* London: DfES. Available at http://webarchive.nationalarchives.gov.uk/20040722013944/dfes.gov.uk/primary document/

DfES (2005) *Key Stage 2 Framework for Languages.* Part 1 and Part 2. London: DfES Publications.

Driscoll, P., Jones, J. and Macrory, G. (2004) *The Provision of Foreign Language Learning for Pupils at Key Stage 2,* DfES Research Report 572. Nottingham: DfES Publications.

Evans, M. and Fisher, L. (2009) *Language Learning at Key Stage 3 – The Impact of the Key Stage 3 Modern Foreign Language Framework and Changes to the Curriculum on Provision and Practice.* Research Report No. RR091 DCSF: London.

Evans, M. and Fisher, L. (2012) 'Emergent communities of practice: secondary schools' interaction with primary school foreign language teaching and learning'. *The Language Learning Journal,* 40(2), 157–173.

Hunt, M., Barnes, A., Powell, B., Lindsay, G. and Mujis, D. (2005) 'Primary modern foreign languages: An overview of recent research, key issues and challenges for educational policy and practice'. *Research Papers in Education,* 20(4), 371–390.

Jones, J. and McLachlan, A. (2009) *Primary Languages in Practice – a Guide to Teaching and Learning.* Berkshire: Open University Press McGraw-Hill.

Muñoz, C. (ed.) (2006) *Age and the Rate of Foreign Language Learning.* Clevedon: Multilingual Matters.

OFSTED (2008) *Primary Languages in Initial Teacher Education.* Reference Number 070031, London: OFSTED.

The Nuffield Foundation (2000) *Languages: The Next Generation.* The Final report and recommendations. London: The Nuffield Foundation.

Rose, J. (2009) *Independent Review of the Primary Curriculum: Final Report.* London: DCSF. https://www.education.gov.uk/publications/eOrderingDownload/Primary_curriculum_Report.pdf

Wade, P., Marshall, H. and O'Donnell, S. (2009) *Primary Modern Foreign Languages Longitudinal Survey of Implementation of National Entitlement to Language learning at Key Stage 2.* National Foundation for Educational Research, Research Report DCSF-RR127. London: DSCF.

Chapter 13

Making a diversified and inclusive language curriculum work

From principles into practice

JIM ANDERSON

BY THE END OF THIS CHAPTER YOU SHOULD:

- recognise the rationale behind a diversified Languages curriculum in secondary schools;
- understand the pedagogical issues arising from a diversified Languages curriculum.

TOWARDS A DIVERSIFIED FLS CURRICULUM

Increasing global interdependence combined with greater recognition of diversity within British society has led to significant shifts in language policy over the past decade (DfES, 2002 and 2007; Ofsted, 2008). Thus we have seen renewed efforts to diversify the range of languages taught in both state maintained and independent schools, as well as greater recognition of the large number of languages taught in the voluntary, community-based 'complementary' sector[1] (CILT *et al.*, 2007–2009). This chapter looks at the pedagogical issues and opportunities raised by these changes which need to be addressed seriously if we are to provide the foundation for a better integrated and more inclusive approach to the learning of other languages.

Readers need to be aware that the term 'community languages' is used in the chapter to refer to languages spoken by minority groups in Britain.[2] The term is problematic, on the one hand, because many languages are taught both as foreign and as community languages (Mandarin being an obvious example), and, on the other hand, because of the negative connotations it carries in the minds of some. We use it here to emphasise the different relationship that learners of 'community languages' have to the language and associated culture as well as ways in which their pedagogical needs are different.

PEDAGOGICAL IMPLICATIONS OF A DIVERSIFIED LANGUAGES CURRICULUM

Shifts in the language teaching landscape identified above have prompted a reassessment of issues of pedagogy centring on two key questions:

1   Are there important distinctions in approach that need to be made between the teaching of the commonly taught European languages and languages of the wider world such as Arabic and Mandarin?

2   Are there further adaptations that need to be made when teaching students who have a background in the language and related culture (community language learners) compared with those who don't (foreign language learners)?

In relation to the first of these questions, whilst it is true that every language has its own distinct features, the 'linguistic distance' (James, 1979) separating the commonly taught European languages from English, is significantly smaller than with languages such as Arabic and Mandarin which are less closely related.[3]

Pedagogically speaking, this has a number of significant implications. Firstly, achieving good pronunciation may be more challenging, particularly in the case of Mandarin where not only sounds but also tones are all important. Teachers need to be skilled in sensitising students' ears to fine distinctions in sound and then in enabling them to produce these correctly. Use of the romanised 'pinyin' system to which diacritic markers can be added to indicate tone levels is one means used to support learners in recognising and producing correct tones. Can you think of other techniques teachers might use to achieve this?

Secondly, since these languages, from an etymological perspective, have less in common with English than is the case with French, German and Spanish, there are fewer cognates that students can rely on in building their vocabulary and accessing the meaning of oral and written texts. What might be the implications of this in the early stages in particular, for example in relation to language input?

Thirdly, both Arabic and Mandarin are written in a different script. Arabic has an alphabet made up of 28 letters most of which change in form depending on whether they occur at the beginning, middle or end of a word, or on their own. However, there is a close correspondence between the written form and the language sounds that it represents. Arabic is written from right to left. Written Chinese is based on a logographic system in which characters provide limited clues to pronunciation, at least for beginners. Learners need to develop an understanding of the internal structure of characters and the stroke order in which characters are written. Achieving basic literacy requires the memorisation of around 3000 characters. How does this affect approaches to reading and writing? Should teachers focus on the development of basic oral skills before literacy is introduced? What steps need to be followed in the introduction of the written form? What strategies can be employed to assist students in recognising and then producing the written form? The need for repeated practice is clear, but are there ways in which this can be made less arduous? Moreover, once basic skills have been achieved, how can students be encouraged to persevere? These are some of the questions faced by teachers of Arabic and Mandarin.

Task 13.1

Pedagogical questions for teachers of arabic and mandarin

Can you think of ways in which these questions might be addressed? For useful guidance here refer to Everson and Xiao (2008).

A further challenge in relation to Arabic relates to its diglossic nature. The written or 'high' form of the language (Modern Standard Arabic) is substantially different from the colloquial, spoken form used in everyday communication, which itself has a number of regional variants. An overemphasis on the written form of the language is likely to mean that students will be unprepared for everyday communication when they visit an Arab country and this could have a demotivating effect. Equally oracy-related work needs to take account of the range of variants across the Arab world and the subtle adjustments required for different social situations.

Task 13.2

Pedagogical questions for teachers of Arabic

Should a choice be made as to which form of the language to teach or is it preferable to adopt a more integrated, diglossic approach emphasising links rather than differences between the two forms as well as contexts of use? What are the implications here for the way Arabic is taught at different stages? What issues arise in preparing students for formal examinations? There are differing views on these matters (Wahba *et al.*, 2006; Omar, 2012).

Try to speak with teachers of Arabic about their approach.

Hitherto we have focussed on aspects of Arabic and Chinese, which present greater challenges for English background students than the commonly taught European languages. However, it should also be remembered that there are some respects in which they may be considered easier. This applies, for example, to aspects of grammar. Chinese verbs don't conjugate and don't change according to tense. Whilst verbs in Arabic do conjugate, the system is very regular.

More broadly it should be mentioned that motivational factors also play a significant role in the value students attach to learning a language and, therefore, the effort that they are prepared to make in their study. Both Arabic and Mandarin are recognised as important world languages, which it may be useful to know for vocational as well as cultural and social reasons. For Muslims, the Arabic language has a particular religious significance and this provides both a sense of cultural affinity, which teachers can draw upon, and a greater incentive for learning it.

Task 13.3

Deciding which language(s) to offer

How should schools decide which language(s) to offer within the curriculum (main and/or extended)? Rank the following criteria in order of the importance you attach to each:

Political and economic

- Widely spoken and high status language (one of six United Nations languages)
- Language of the European Union

Academic/Vocational

- Asset in future study and/or career

Intellectual and historical

- Training of the mind. Foundation for learning other European languages. Origins of Western civilisation. (Greek and Latin)

Linguistic and pedagogical

- More closely related to English making it easier to guess meanings (origins, script)

Social and cultural

- Significant number of pupils have a background in the language and culture and opportunity to use it in everyday life (accelerated learning)
- Raises students' self-esteem and supports community cohesion

Practical

- Availability of qualified teachers
- Availability of resources

So far we have looked at features of Arabic and Mandarin, which are different in significant ways from commonly taught European languages, and begun to consider what the implications might be for pedagogy. We now move on to the second of the questions set out at the beginning of this chapter related not so much to the language itself as to the relationship of learners to the language. More precisely, what factors do teachers working with community language learners need to take account of and how should this affect their approach to pedagogy?

Crucially, it needs to be understood that these learners cover a very wide spectrum in terms of competence and have abilities which typically are skewed towards oracy and listening skills in particular (Anderson, 2008). Teachers need to find out where students' strengths and weaknesses lie and to ensure that activities are pitched appropriately, extending rather than repeating what is already known. In order to encourage a harmonious and supportive classroom atmosphere, having students work around a common theme or text is considered a desirable aim. This means that there can be phases within lessons or sequences of lessons where students can work together even though they may be carrying out tasks at different levels for some of the time. Refer to Convery and Coyle (2009) and Anderson and Chung (2011b, Chapter 4) for further strategies that can be drawn upon to support differentiation.

With regard to input of language, starting at the most basic level by teaching vocabulary and structures through the stepped, three-stage questioning technique, commonly used in the FL classroom, is likely to be less effective with community language students who may easily feel bored or even insulted by such an approach. In order to refresh and extend existing knowledge, teachers in community language classrooms commonly use brainstorming techniques around a theme or question supported by a visual stimulus. This enables the development and organisation of ideas and language, allows a smooth transition to be made from spoken to written forms and can incorporate reference skills. In the case of languages such as Arabic and Bengali, where there are significant differences between colloquial regional varieties and standard forms, brainstorming allows awareness of these differences to be built up, but teachers need to be skilled in handling this in ways that do not undermine students' confidence.

Another useful approach is through collaborative work around texts (Lunzer and Gardner, 1984; Wray and Lewis, 1997) which again can bridge oral and written modes and can accommodate learners with differing levels of competence as well as different learning styles. There are a number of activities that can be useful here (See Task 13.4 below).

Task 13.4

Collaborative work around texts

Choose a text suitable for a pre-GCSE class in a language you are familiar with. It may, for example, be a short article, a poem or a dialogue. Select two 'reconstruction' and two 'analysis' activities from the list below that you consider would be appropriate for the text chosen. Note down the reasons for your choice. Create the activities indicating high (***), average (**) or low (*) level of challenge involved. Try out with a class divided into groups of three and observe levels of engagement and thinking.

Reconstruction

- gap-fill (filling in missing words/phrases)
- sequencing (arranging scrambled segments of text into logical order)
- table completion (referring to text to fill in information under headings in a table)
- prediction (discussing and/or writing the next stage or ending of a text)

Analysis

- text marking (underlining or highlighting parts of text containing certain meaning or information, e.g. key ideas, lexical or grammatical categories)
- text segmenting and labelling (matching images or headings to paragraphs)
- diagram construction (recasting information in diagrammatic form, e.g. as mind map, time line, flow chart)
- question setting (making up questions on the text – to be answered by peers)
- paraphrasing and summarising (putting a passage from text into own words /identifying key ideas and expressing them clearly and concisely)

These techniques can easily be applied to work with stories, which often feature in the community language classroom for cultural as well as linguistic reasons. Stories can provide a valuable springboard into a range of creative work by learners involving art work, drama, dance and multimedia (Sneddon, 2009; Anderson and Chung, 2011a and b; Datta, 2007). Importantly, this can allow reinterpretation of traditional or contemporary material in terms of students' own lives, challenging static, essentialised notions of culture and encouraging students to draw on and develop perspectives which reflect their bilingual–bicultural identities. Such work, which provides cognitive challenge and prioritises learner agency, is captured in Cummins' term 'identity texts' (2006: 60), which are seen as especially empowering for community language learners because they 'hold a mirror up to students in which their identities are reflected back in a positive light'.

Drawing on the arts is one way to enrich curriculum content and to provide a context for the development of intercultural skills in the teaching of community and FLs. Another approach, which has attracted much interest in recent years both in the context of FL learning and community/heritage language learning, is Content and Language Integrated Learning (CLIL), also known as immersion teaching (Coyle, Holmes and King, 2009; Coyle, Hood and Marsh, 2010; Meier, 2010). As with the EAL learner who has achieved some degree of conversational fluency, the priority for the community/heritage language learner is to develop the ability to use language for a wider range of cognitive functions across the spectrum of spoken and written genres (Christian, 2008; Anderson, 2009). This may relate to the teaching of a particular subject through the medium of the community language or to broader cross-curricular 'thematic' teaching approaches which can also address citizenship issues (Anderson and Chaudhuri, 2003). From the teacher's standpoint this involves a shift in approach when planning lessons. Instead of focussing mainly or entirely on the language that is being taught, priority has to be given to the knowledge, understanding and skills related to the subject(s) covered. It is also important for teachers to be highly proficient in the range of scaffolding strategies which enable learners to engage with more challenging content. These include the active reading and writing strategies referred to above.

An issue that has raised much interest recently in the context of community language classrooms, but which has also been an on-going subject of debate amongst teachers of FLs for decades, has to do with use of the target language (TL) and whether, instead of banning use of English from the classroom, a more flexible bilingual approach might be beneficial (Creese and Blackledge, 2010; Hall and Cook, 2012). Part of the rationale for the more flexible approach is that it challenges monolingual assumptions through which languages are viewed as separate entities and recognises learners' status as bilinguals, valuing their bilingual skills rather than seeking to aspire to native speaker norms – a 'multi-competency' model (Cook, 2008, pp. 231–233). Furthermore, it recognises 'translanguaging' as a natural phenomenon within bilingual communication (Garcia, 2009, pp. 44–51). On the other hand, from a pedagogical standpoint, overuse of English may encourage dependency and hinder the development of important communication skills in the TL.

Another important and related area here is the development of learners' meta-linguistic awareness, encouraging them to understand commonalities as well as differences between languages and to develop deeper insights into language learning (Edwards, 2009; Kenner, 2000). This tends to occur naturally where students are encouraged to draw on the full range of their language skills in researching and carrying out tasks which involve different languages. Opportunities here include referring to information in one language and responding in another, giving a presentation bilingually and creating bilingual books. In Wales, where Welsh and English as well as a FL are taught in many schools, the benefits of an integrated and inclusive approach to literacy development have been understood and acted upon (Welsh Government, 2011). Similar approaches to literacy aiming to build links across different language specialisms have also been developed through 'language awareness' work (Hawkins, 1984; Anderson, 1991; Datta and Pomphrey, 2004; CILT/Goldsmiths, University of London, 2011) which has gained fresh impetus recently through the development of primary languages.

Whilst there is a need for understandings of literacy to be extended beyond English to take account of other languages, it has also become increasingly apparent that the association of literacy with writing or print needs to be expanded to take account of the ever-increasing significance of multimodal communication in the modern world (Allford and Pachler, 2007; Pahl and Rowsell, 2012). This presents new pedagogical challenges, but also new opportunities for language learning, especially in relation to the less widely taught languages where finding appropriate, up-to-date teaching resources has been a long-standing issue. The possibilities opened up here relate to important elements within second language learning methodology including input/output, social interaction, authenticity, exposure, feedback and learner autonomy. (Anderson, 2001; Cummins, Brown and Sayers, 2007; Anderson and Chung, 2011b: Chapter 10).

SUMMARY

In this chapter we have considered pedagogical issues arising from the teaching of languages other than the commonly taught European languages (French, German and Spanish). We have also looked at factors which need to be taken into account when working with learners who have a background in the language/culture as opposed to those who are learning it from a FL perspective. Whilst these pedagogical matters are of most immediate concern to teachers, it is important that Heads of Department and curriculum managers, as well as policy makers at local and national levels, have an awareness of them too. Thus far National Curriculum documents and other official frameworks for the teaching of languages have focussed almost entirely on the commonly taught European languages. This eurocentric and exclusive policy based on monolingual assumptions undermines teachers' efforts to provide high quality language teaching and to engage with wider literacy and citizenship agendas.

NOTES

1   Complementary schools are also referred to as 'supplementary', 'mother tongue' and 'weekend' schools.

2   Community languages are also referred to as 'heritage' languages and this is the preferred term in the United States and Canada.

3   Arabic and Chinese are the two languages referred to most frequently in this chapter. However, many of the issues referred to in relation to them are also relevant, to a greater or lesser extent, to the wide range of other languages taught in our schools.

REFERENCES

Allford, D. and Pachler, N. (2007) *Language, Autonomy and New Learning Environments*. Frankfurt a. M.: Peter Lang.

Anderson. J. (1991) 'The potential of Language Awareness as a focus for cross-curricular work in the secondary sector', in James, C. and Garrett, P. (eds) *Language Awareness in the Classroom*. London: Longman, pp. 133–139.

Anderson. J. (2001) 'ICT and community languages: insights from a web publishing project', in *Reflections on ICT*. London: CILT, pp. 30–40.

Anderson. J. and Chaudhuri, M. (2003) 'Citizenship and community languages: a critical perspective', in *Reflections on Citizenship in a Multilingual World*. London: CILT, pp. 53–65.

Anderson, J. (2008) 'Towards integrated second language teaching pedagogy for foreign and community/heritage languages in multilingual Britain'. *Language Learning Journal*, 36(1), 79–89.

Anderson, J. (2009) 'Relevance of CLIL in developing pedagogies for minority language teaching', in Marsh, D., Meehisto, P., Wolff, D., Aliaga, R., Asiakinen, T., Frigols-Martin, M. J., Hughes, S. and Lange, G. (eds) *CLIL Practice: Perspectives from the Field*. University of Jyväskylä (Finland): CCN, pp. 124–132.

Anderson, J. and Chung, Y-C. (2011a) 'Finding a voice: arts based creativity in the community languages classroom'. *International Journal of Bilingual Education and Bilingualism*, 14(5), 551–569.

Anderson, J. and Chung, Y-C. (2011b) *Arts Based Creativity in the Community Languages Classroom: a Professional Development Resource*. London: Goldsmiths, University of London. http://www.gold.ac.uk/clcl/multilingual-learning/creativity/booklet/#d.en.26692

Christian, D. (2008) 'School-based programs for heritage language learners: two-way immersion', in Brinton, D., Kagan, O. and Bauckus, S. (eds) *Heritage Language Education: A New Field Emerging*. New York: Routledge, pp. 257–268.

CILT, the National Centre for Languages: Primary Languages http://www.primarylanguages.org.uk/teaching__learning/ict.aspx (Accessed September 2012).

CILT, the National Centre for Languages, National Resource Centre for Supplementary Education, Specialist Schools and Academies Trust and School Development Support Agency (2007–2009) *Our Languages project*. http://www.ourlanguages.org.uk/

CILT, the National Centre for Languages/Goldsmiths, University of London (2011) *Initial Teacher Training Modules for Teaching Community Languages in Primary Schools*. London: CILT, the National Centre for Languages. http://www.primarylanguages.org.uk/teaching__learning/community_languages/professional_development.aspx

Convery, A. and Coyle, D. (2009) *Finding the Right Fit*. (Classic Pathfinder). London: CILT.

Cook, V. J. (2008) *Second Language Learning and Language Teaching*. 4th edition. London: Hodder Education.

Coyle, D., Holmes, B. and King, L. (2009) *CLIL National Statement and Guidelines*. London: The Languages Company.

Coyle, D., Hood, P. and Marsh, D. (2010) *CLIL: Content and Language Integrated Learning*. Cambridge: CUP.

Creese, A. and Blackledge, A. (2010) 'Translanguaging in the bilingual classroom: a pedagogy for learning and teaching?' *The Modern Language Journal*, 94(1), 103–115.

Cummins, J. (2006) 'Identity texts: The imaginative construction of self through multiliteracies of pedagogy', in García, O., Skutnabb-Kangas, T. and Torres-Guzmán, M. (eds) *Imagining Multilingual Schools. Language in Education and Globalization*. Clevedon: Multilingual Matters, pp. 51–68.

Cummins, J., Brown, K. and Sayers, D. (2007) *Literacy, Technology, and Diversity: Teaching for Success in Changing Times*. Boston: Pearson.

Datta, M. and Pomphrey, C. (2004) *A World of Languages – Developing Children's Love of Languages*. London: CILT.

Datta, M. (ed.) (2007) *Bilinguality and Literacy: Principles and Practice*. 2nd edition. London: Continuum.

DfES (2002) *Languages for All: Languages for Life*. London: DfES. https://www.education.gov.uk/publications/eOrderingDownload/DfESLanguages Strategy.pdf

DfES (2007) *Languages Review*. London: DfES. https://www.education.gov.uk/publications/standard/publicationDetail/Page1/DFES-00212-2007

Edwards, V. (2009) *Learning to be Literate: Multilingual Perspectives*. Bristol: Multilingual Matters.

Everson, M. E. and Xiao, Y (eds) (2008) *Teaching Chinese As a Foreign Language: Theories and Applications*. Boston: Cheng & Tsui.

Garcia, O. (2009) *Bilingual Education in the 21st Century: A Global Perspective*. Chichester, West Sussex: Wiley-Blackwell.

Hall, G. and Cook, G. (2012) 'Own-language use in language teaching and learning', in *Language Teaching*, 45(3), 271–308.

Hawkins, E. (1984) *Awareness of Language: An Introduction*. Cambridge: Cambridge University Press.

James, C. (1979) 'Foreign Languages in the school curriculum', in Perren, G. (ed.) *Foreign Languages in Education*, NCLE Papers and Reports. London: CILT.

Kenner, C. (2000) *Home Pages: Literacy Links for Bilingual Children*. Stoke-on-Trent: Trentham Books.

Lunzer, E. A. and Gardner, K. (1984) *Learning from the Written Word*. Edinburgh: Oliver and Boyd.

Meier, G. (2010) 'Two-way immersion programmes in Germany: Bridging the linguistic gap'. *International Journal of Bilingual Education and Bilingualism*, 13(4), 419–437.

Ofsted (2008) *Every Language Matters*. http://www.ofsted.gov.uk/

Omar, Y. (2012) *Teaching Arabic to Speakers of Other Languages: Theory and Practice*. London: London Arabic Publications.

Pahl, K. and Rowsell, J. (2012) *Literacy and Education: Understanding the New Literacy Studies in the Classroom.* 2nd edition. London: Sage Publications.

Sneddon, R. (2009) *Bilingual Books – Biliterate Children: Learning to Read through Dual Language Books.* Stoke-on-Trent: Trentham.

Wahba, K. M., Taha, Z. A. and England, L. (2006) *Handbook for Arabic Language Teaching Professionals in the 21st Century.* Mahwah, New Jersey: Lawrence Erlbaum.

Welsh Government (2011) *Supporting Triple Literacy: Language learning in Key Stage 2 and Key Stage 3.* Cardiff: Welsh Government. http://wales.gov.uk/docs/dcells/publications/111017literacyen.pdf

Wray, D. and Lewis, M. (1997) *Extending Literacy: Children Reading and Writing Non-fiction.* London: Routledge.

CURRICULUM GUIDES

Saffaf, S. and Abdel-Hay, N. (2007) *Curriculum Guide for Arabic.* London: CILT, The National Centre for Languages.
http://www.gold.ac.uk/clcl/multilingual-learning/curriculumguides/

Thompson, A., Lee, E. and Li, K. (2007) *Curriculum Guide for Chinese.* London: CILT, The National Centre for Languages.
http://www.gold.ac.uk/clcl/multilingual-learning/curriculumguides/

Chandla, N. and Grewal, P. (2007) *Curriculum Guide for Panjabi.* London: CILT, The National Centre for Languages.
http://www.gold.ac.uk/clcl/multilingual-learning/curriculumguides/

Pillai, S. and Nithiya, K. (2007) *Curriculum Guide for Tamil.* London: CILT, The National Centre for Languages.
http://www.gold.ac.uk/clcl/multilingual-learning/curriculumguides/

Ali, K. and Syed, H. (2007) *Curriculum Guide for Urdu.* London: CILT, The National Centre for Languages.
http://www.gold.ac.uk/clcl/multilingual-learning/curriculumguides/

Bhatt, A. and Kant, J. (2009) *Curriculum Guide for Gujarati.* CILT, The National Centre for Languages.

Brook, C., Lee, E. and Li, K. (2009) *Curriculum Guide for Chinese (Cantonese).* London: CILT, The National Centre for Languages.

Farah, Y. and Mohamud, A. (2009) *Curriculum Guide for Somali.* London: CILT, The National Centre for Languages.

Oyetade, A. and Oke, Y. (2009) *Curriculum Guide for Yoruba.* CILT, The National Centre for Languages.

SOME USEFUL WEBSITES

Association of Language Learning: Special Interest Group for World Languages
http://www.alllanguages.org.uk/community/committees_and_sigs/list_of_committees_and_sigs/special_interest_group_for_world_languages

The Bilingual Immersion Education Network (BIEN)
www.bien.org.uk

Critical Connections: Multilingual Digital Storytelling Project (Goldsmiths, University of London)
http://goldsmithsmdst.wordpress.com/

Dual Language Books
http://www.uel.ac.uk/duallanguagebooks/what.htm

Fostering a Love of Languages: The Language Futures Toolkit
http://www.phf.org.uk/page.asp?id=1854

Home Languages Accreditation Project (HOLA) (Languages Sheffield)
http://www.languages-sheffield.org.uk/hda-project/hda-project

Language Box
http://languagebox.ac.uk/
Multilingual Learning (Goldsmiths, University of London)
http://www.gold.ac.uk/clcl/multilingual-learning/

National Association for Language Development in the Curriculum
http://www.naldic.org.uk/

National Resource Centre for Supplementary Education
http://www.continyou.org.uk/what_we_do/children_and_young_people/
supplementary_education

Our Languages
http://www.ourlanguages.org.uk/

Waltham Forest Bilingual Group
http://www.wfbilingual.org.uk/

Chapter 14 · Working with other adults in the foreign languages classroom

ANA REDONDO

BY THE END OF THIS CHAPTER YOU SHOULD:

- understand the policy context governing the work of teaching assistants (TAs);
- have become familiar with key research findings from the field; and
- be able to apply this understanding in your work with support staff, in particular TAs and Foreign Language Assistants (FLAs).

THE POLICY CONTEXT

In 2003, a historic national agreement was reached between the then Labour government, employers and school workforce unions to implement new models of teaching and learning in response to a perceived need for innovation in the area of contractual arrangements for the school workforce. Unrelenting reform and innovation had brought, and continues to bring with it, increasing pressure on teachers' time resulting from non-teaching activities, and there was a perceived need for reducing excessive workloads and for remodelling the workforce with wide-ranging implications for teaching and non-teaching staff (see DfES *et al.*, 2003). Under the so-called remodelling agenda, support staff saw their roles expanded and they were increasingly recognised for the contribution they make to the education of young people, be it in their capacity as administrative, technical or, most importantly for our present discussion, as classroom support staff. For teachers this meant an aspiration that they should not routinely do administrative and clerical tasks and have support so that they can focus on teaching and learning. By implication, support staff were being asked to take on an increasing range of duties and responsibilities. For both parties these changes in the conceptualisation of their roles and responsibilities make close collaboration not only desirable but necessary. For a discussion, see e.g. Bedford, Jackson and Wilson (2008).

TAs became headline news in 2013 when the Treasury and the Department of Education of the Coalition government were considering to reduce their number considerably in a seeming attempt to reverse the workforce remodelling agenda of the Labour government to free up funds to increase the number of teachers. Research was being used to justify an attempted saving of £4 billion a year.

WHAT THE RESEARCH SAYS

Press coverage and related policy advice, reporting and reflecting on research by Peter Blatchford and colleagues (2004; 2012), focused on the finding that pupils who receive support from TAs make less progress than peers of similar ability who don't. The research also shows that TAs bring benefits in terms of teachers' workload, stress and job satisfaction as well as in terms of enabling individualized attention, increasing the amount of teaching and minimizing 'off-task' behaviour (Webster, Russel and Blatchford, 2009); alas, these benefits tended not to be reported by the press. In a recent blog post (http://ioelondonblog.wordpress.com/category/peter-blatchford), Blatchford points out that it is important how one interprets the results. In particular, he points to the importance of how TAs are used in schools and how they are prepared for their work, and that the findings of his research suggests that TAs tend not to be used 'to the best advantage' often despite the best intentions of schools:

> Often TAs, with little preparation or training, are assigned a one-to-one remedial role with low attaining pupils or those with special educational needs (SEN). We suggest that this is misguided and helps explain the negative impact on these pupils.

He concludes that a reduction in the number of TAs is a bad idea.

Together with his colleagues, he developed the so-called Wider Pedagogical Role (WPR) model (see Russell, Webster and Blatchford, 2013, p. 2) comprising the following three components:

> First, there is the *preparedness* of TAs and teachers, which covers: (i) their training for their respective roles (for teachers this will influence how they make the most of TAs in their classrooms, and for TAs, training will influence their pedagogical and subject understanding); and, (ii) the amount of planning, preparation and debriefing/feedback time available for teachers and TAs. The second component, the *deployment* of TAs by teachers and headteachers, concerns which pupils TAs are allocated to work with; typically, this will be individuals and groups of lower-attaining pupils and those with SEN. And finally, the *practice* of TAs concerns the nature and quality of their interactions with pupils, which we found to be far less academically demanding and task-driven, compared with teacher-to-pupil interactions.

Russell *et al.* argue that, together, these factors enable the most fruitful insights into the effectiveness of the learning support provided by TAs.

In a paper reporting on a related project exploring the effective deployment of TAs, the researchers (Webster, Blatchford and Russell, 2013, pp. 90) discuss inter alia features of TA-to-pupil talk and stress the ineffectiveness of the following types of talk:

- closing down talk (e.g. closed questions and leading statements; supplying answers);
- emphasising task completion rather than learning and understanding;
- 'stereo teaching' (e.g. repeating, more or less exactly, teacher talk, moments after teacher has spoken);
- providing inaccurate or vague explanations of instructions, processes and concepts.

For a detailed discussion of interactions of TAs with pupils see Rubie-Davies, Blatchford and Webster, 2010, who conclude that TAs are not teachers and that not the same should be expected of them. They ask whether TAs should be used directly in teaching roles, including as that of primary educator for supported pupils, or whether, instead, they should contribute to other aspects such as to encourage pupil motivation and classroom organization and management. If deemed to have a pedagogical contribution to make, they argue that attention is required as to what constitutes appropriate forms of pedagogical TA deployment and that these need to be made explicit. (p. 446)

Task 14.1

Defining roles and responsibilities

Defining roles and responsibilities of teachers and support staff is an important first step in ensuring effective collaboration with TAs.
Consider the following questions:

- How do you think pupils' learning can be maximised by the presence of a TA in your foreign language (FL) lessons?
- What expectations do you have of a TA's presence in your lesson? What would you expect in terms of his/her contribution?
- How would you consider involving him/her?
- What expertise would you expect him/her to have?

List the respective responsibilities you think TAs can carry out in FL education and how you can best support them in discharging them. It might be helpful to use the following four categories to structure your deliberations:

- support for the pupil;
- support for the teacher;
- support for the curriculum;
- support for the school.

This chapter explores the implications of these important changes for FL teachers. Managing the contribution of the TA in the classroom is, therefore, of crucial importance.

FROM POLICY TO PRACTICE

For FL educators the issues involved in working with other adults in the classroom are far from new and ostensibly provide an opportunity to consolidate existing practice going on in many classrooms up and down the country, who have benefited from FLAs for some time (since 1905 in the UK in fact) and other native speakers routinely deployed, in order to bring pupils in closer contact with the target language and culture and its speakers. For specific guidance on working with FLAs see e.g. Pachler, Evans, Redondo and Fisher, 2014.

TAs either work with a whole class or support individual or small groups of children. In secondary schools, TAs have traditionally tended to work as special needs assistants supporting pupils with learning difficulties, a practice – as we have seen earlier – research has shown to be sub-optimal if not managed appropriately by the teacher. They are increasingly working as specialists for a subject and contribute to lesson planning, the development of support materials or class supervision duties.

The activities of this chapter focus on working with other support staff, in particular TAs, through a range of practical activities in the areas of planning and evaluation (Task 14.2), lesson behaviour management (Task 14.3), assessment (Task 14.4) and, of course, professional development (Task 14.5).

Task 14.2

Planning

Imagine you teach a class of 30 mixed ability Year 9 pupils. You have included three activities with several tasks to be completed within each of these in your lesson plan ranging from simple to more complex. The lesson lasts for one hour in which pupils will get a chance to practise speaking, listening and responding and reading comprehension. A TA usually attends your lessons with this group.

Here are a series of questions for you to consider:

- How would you approach your lesson? Will you ask the TA to support one or more pupils taking his own initiative? Will you talk to him/her about the activities that will take place in the lesson? If so, when will you do so and why? Will you hand out a lesson plan with specific instructions and guidelines? What are the relative advantages of these approaches?
- Do you think that the TA would immediately understand the purpose of the different activities you are intending to carry out in your lesson? Would he be able to predict and support how the learners are going to approach and carry out the tasks? Should you be planning lessons together? What are the advantages and disadvantages?
- Is it essential that the TA is familiar with, and understands well the outcomes you want to achieve? If so, how would you find out that the TA actually understands the outcomes you are trying to achieve?
- How can you ascertain whether or not a TA is effective at supporting the learners? Is it enough for you to judge by the way you see him/her interacting with one or several pupils in the course of the lesson? What can you do to ensure that the TA's contribution to the lesson is most effective?
- Do you consider it valuable to meet with a TA you share lessons with on a regular basis? If so, would you meet during your non-contact time or after school? What do you consider to be the best use of time for these meetings? Order the following items in order of priority for your meetings with the TA:
  - planning time is the best time spent with a TA;
  - teaching the TA the meaning and the pronunciation of the vocabulary to be presented in lessons;
  - coaching the TA on how best to support pupils who will be completing some reading comprehension tasks;
  - asking the TA to prepare a drama activity which a small group will perform to their peers.
- What might be likely constraints you could encounter in your own practice in the light of all the questions above?

In the same way it is desirable to engage in joint planning with TAs, you should carry out lesson evaluations jointly with TAs with whom you share lessons. What are the implications for your planning of subsequent lesson(s) and your medium-term planning with the group you both share?

As part of a practical approach to joint planning and evaluation with the TA, this proforma might be useful:

Unit of work:		Lesson topic:	
Teaching group:			
Number of lesson in unit:			
Number of pupils in class: M … / F … SEN … EAL …			
Objective(s), language content (lexis, forms, functions, culture) and language learning skills			
	Teacher	TA	Pupils
Main activities and tasks incl. homework:			
Materials, resources and equipment:			
Individual/groups to work with TA:			
Review of teaching and learning by teacher:			
Feedback from TA on the learning of individual pupils and the lesson as a whole:			
Points/targets for next lesson:			

Task 14.3

Behaviour management

How can your behaviour management strategies take into account any contribution a TA makes to your lessons?

How would you define the role of the TA in relation to discipline in your lessons? How appropriate do you consider the following to be? The TA:

- giving verbal warnings to individual pupils;
- setting detentions for after school which s/he will supervise;
- writing a letter home to parents/carers;
- approaching the pupil's form tutor in order to discuss the child's behaviour in FLs lessons;
- telephoning parents/carers to inform them of the pupil's detention;
- telephoning parents/carers to inform them of their child's poor behaviour;
- discussing with the head of department some steps to follow in order to deal with the poor behaviour of a pupil/pupils in a lesson;
- informing the head of department of the action s/he has taken after an incident of poor behaviour in a lesson with a copy to the teacher whose lesson the TA was working in.

What actions, if any, do you think are definitely outside the remit of the TA's role and responsibility within the classroom and lessons you both share?

Discuss your answers with an experienced colleague in school.

Task 14.4

Assessment

Assessment is another key area of work. What contribution can a TA make to it? How appropriate are the statements below? TAs:

- should be assessing pupils' work in a variety of skills;
- should carry out marking exercise books;
- might be helpful in assisting pupils in using bilingual dictionaries;
- can help pupils with learning difficulties to copy the vocabulary in their exercise book and ensure that copying is accurate;
- best work with pupils on a one-to-one basis for error correction and feedback;
- should take pupils outside the lesson to work with them to improve their work;
- should prepare specific assessment tasks for those pupils with learning difficulties who they support;
- should concentrate on assessing and supporting only those pupils who they are assigned to, in particular those with learning difficulties;
- should not carry out any whole-class assessment activities;
- can take the register and make notes in the teacher's mark book.

You might wish to discuss them with a colleague.

Task 14.5

Continuing professional development

In terms of CPD, consider the following questions:

- What areas of your teaching could be improved by working with TAs in your lesson?
- In what way do you think you can play a role in a TA's professional development?

THE QUESTION OF LINGUISTIC COMPETENCE

If TAs are to be effective in FLs lessons, they need to have some basic competence in the language taught. TAs might have a background or basic qualifications in a FL. Nevertheless, it is likely that they will benefit from refreshing or further developing their skills and communicative competence in the FL in order to have enough language and cultural knowledge to be able to complement your work in lessons effectively. It is only right to expect that TAs should attend some courses which provide them with skills and competences that can make their contribution in the FL classroom more effective. Language enhancement courses are likely to be available externally, but the FLs department also needs to make sure relevant pedagogical support is available in-house in the same way many departments provide in-house training and support for FLs teachers.

Some knowledge of a language by the TA can go a long way towards assisting pupils in their FL learning. Together with the requisite basic pedagogical skills it can allow for a real partnership between the teacher and the TA. For instance, when activities are set out by the teacher in a lesson and clear instructions are given about how to carry out the tasks in hand, TAs are in a good position to guide and support pupils in a one-to-one situation or in group work activities to carry out and successfully complete the work.

When defining strategies which can help young people learn a FL, such as memorising, grasping grammatical concepts, practising language, language drills and a whole host of other FL tasks, TAs can enable learners to remain focused and on-task and feel they can ask for the help they individually require without having to wait unnecessarily long stretches until the teacher is available to do so.

Whilst there are no hard and fast rules for how to work alongside a TA, there are some practices, which should help maximise the benefits to be derived from additional adult attention. These include:

- do not feel threatened to use the expertise available;
- establish good lines of communication;
- establish a collegial atmosphere characterized by mutual trust;
- establish clear roles and responsibilities;
- regularly review the effectiveness of collaborative practices;
- demonstrate that you value your TA.

SUMMARY

FLs teachers have a long tradition of working with other adults inside and outside the classroom. As the number of adults other than teachers in schools and classrooms has increased, with it has the need to adapt approaches to teaching and learning to maximise the benefits to be derived from them.

REFERENCES

Bedford, D., Jackson, C. and Wilson, E. (2008) 'New partnerships for learning: teachers' perspectives on their developing relationships with teaching assistants in England'. *Journal of In-Service Education*, 34(1), 7–25.

Blatchford, P., Russell, A., Bassett, P., Brown, P. and Martin. C. (2004) *The Role and Effects of Teaching Assistants in English Primary Schools (Years 4 to 6) 2000–2003: Results from the Class Size and Pupil-Adult Ratios (CSPAR) KS2 Project.* DfES Research Report RR605. Available at: http://webarchive.nationalarchives.gov.uk/20130401151715/https://www.education.gov.uk/publications/eOrderingDownload/RR605.pdf

Blatchford, P., Russell, A. and Webster, R. (2012) *Reassessing the Impact of Teaching Assistants: How Research Challenges Practice and Policy.* Abingdon: Routledge.

DfES et al. (2003) *Raising Standards and Tackling Workload: A National Agreement. Time for Standards.* January 15.

Pachler, N., Evans, M., Redondo, A. and Fisher, L. (2014) *Learning to Teach Foreign Languages in the Secondary School.* London: Routledge.

Rubie-Davies, C., Blatchford, P. and Webster, R. (2010) 'Enhancing learning? A comparison of teacher and teaching assistant interactions with pupils'. *School Effectiveness and School Improvement*, 21(4), 429–449.

Russell, A., Webster, R. and Blatchford, P. (2013) *Maximising the Impact of Teaching Assistants: Guidance for School Leaders and Teachers.* Abingdon: Routledge.

Webster, R., Blatchford, P. and Russell, A. (2013) 'Challenging and changing how schools use teaching assistants: findings from the Effective Deployment of Teaching Assistants project', in *School Leadership & Management: Formerly School Organisation* 33(1), pp. 78–96.

Webster, R., Russell, A. and Blatchford, P. (2009) 'A help or a hindrance?' *Every Child Journal*, 1(2), 64–67.

USEFUL WEBSITES AND RESOURCES

British Council online guidance for Foreign Language Assistant http://www. languageassistant.co.uk

Centre international d'études pédagogiques online guidance for Foreign Language Assistant http://www.ciep.fr/en/assistantetr

Chapter 15   Reflective practice through teacher research

MIKE CALVERT

BY THE END OF THIS CHAPTER YOU SHOULD:

- appreciate the importance of, and the need for, reflective practice;
- understand how reflection can form part of your personal and professional development;
- have gained some insights into the value of classroom research;
- have acquired some ideas for using research to inform your practice;
- have learnt more about sources of information to inform your practice.

INTRODUCTION

You are, or aspire to be, an autonomous, well qualified and self-directed teacher or you would not be taking the trouble of reading this book. These are the hallmarks of an extended professional. This chapter sets out to guide you by describing what reflective practice is, explaining how important it can be and suggesting ways in which you can progress in a systematic and sustainable way. Essentially, the chapter argues that a key skill of a professional is the ability to reflect on themselves and their practice and that research offers a powerful vehicle for such reflection and change.

Classrooms are complex places with 'too many moving parts' and our job as teachers is to make sense of what is going on, cope with the dilemmas that we face in the classroom and change what we do accordingly. Rolfe, Freshwater and Jasper (2001) talk of: 'What? So what? Now what? How are you going to make sense of your classroom, exercise judgement and make the changes that will make a difference?'

WHAT IS A REFLECTIVE PRACTITIONER?

In straightforward terms, a reflective practitioner is someone who is consistently questioning their practice and not content to take materials, teaching methods and ideas at their face value but sets out to examine them in their own context and decide what is best for the pupils in light of their reading and knowledge. The reflective practitioner also reflects on his or her own impact on the learning experience. We reflect in two ways: in-action and on-action. In other words, we reflect on our actions in 'real time' but also after the event in lesson evaluations, when we are driving home or marking books.

Ways of reflecting

Respond to the statements below. Identify ways in which you (might) reflect. Tick the appropriate box(es) for each statement.

	I try to do this regularly but it is not always possible.	I would like to do this but never manage to do so.	This is not feasible given my role and responsibilities.	I don't think this is necessary.	I am not currently in a situation where I can do this but I would like to do it.	I'll try to do this in future.
I note down briefly reflections on how the lesson has gone as soon as I can after the lesson.						
At the end of the day, I write up my reflections on the lessons.						
I focus on one class at a time and concentrate on getting that class right.						

I invite others to observe part or all of a lesson in order to get another perspective.					
I am always looking for new ideas in books or websites.					
I go to watch other teachers and learn from them.					
I ask pupils for their opinions and their ideas.					
I visit other schools and find out how they do things.					

(Adapted from Race, 2005)

By the time you have picked up this book, you will have started already to develop a repertoire of approaches and some of them may be so automatic that you use them without thinking. Such craft knowledge has come to you from your own experience as a language learner, from your tutors and mentors, from observation of, and advice from, other teachers and from your reading. In time, we, as teachers, become far more confident in a variety of situations and, with experience, run the risk of being satisfied that we know *where* we are going and *what* we are doing. What we do not always know is *why* we are doing what we are doing and what improvements could be made. Do we understand the underlying theory/theories behind what we are doing? How does theory underpin our practice? There is a lot of truth in the saying that there is nothing as practical as good theory.

WHY BE A REFLECTIVE PRACTITIONER?

As our 'stage act' becomes more routine, it is all too easy to take things for granted and settle for the tried and tested approaches. Our workload may well increase as will the responsibilities that we have. Personal pressures may well encroach and we may too readily slip into patterns which may or may not represent the best learning we can offer.

Task 15.2

Reasons for changing practice

Think about what motivates you as a teacher and what stimulates you to change and improve. Note down what you come up with and compare it with other teachers using the grid below.

	I strongly agree	I agree	Neither agree or disagree	I disagree	I strongly disagree
I am motivated to reflect on my work and improve because I take a pride in my work.					
I rely on my experience and do not need to reflect in detail.					
I have no time to reflect so just get on with it.					
I am motivated to reflect on my work and improve because I am a professional.					

I rely on 'gut reaction' and this serves me well.					
I am motivated to reflect on my work and change because repetition bores me.					
I would reflect if I had time but for now I just get on with doing what I have to do.					
I am motivated to improve because I am afraid to fail.					
I am motivated to reflect and improve because that is what a professional does.					

(Adapted from Race, 2005)

Essentially, the arguments for reflection can be broken down into moral, pedagogical and personal. Morally, as professionals we have a responsibility to update our skills and knowledge and mediate political and educational decisions that affect our situation. Pedagogically, we know that each classroom is different and that context specificity is crucial in adapting and reflecting on what we do with each class. There is no 'silver bullet' for any teaching situation and we must avoid the 'what works' philosophy which appears to suggest that there is one answer. This is questionable and can lead to simplistic assumptions based on cause and effect. At a personal level, we know that we are more enthusiastic and satisfied if we are doing new things and taking on new challenges and can expect to get more out of the students and greater job satisfaction if we engage wholeheartedly in the learning process. Injecting new questions and new ideas is vital. Crudely, do we want to teach for 30 years or for one year 30 times?

HOW CAN YOU REFLECT IN A MORE ORGANISED, SYSTEMATIC WAY?

We all reflect to some degree but that does not necessarily mean that it leads anywhere. Indeed, we can go through life without our reflection bringing any significant change or improvement to our situation. If we are committed to our reflective practice leading to change, we may need a framework or vehicle for our reflection.

Here are some suggestions:

- having regular, timetabled (and sacrosanct) mentoring sessions;
- having a more informal but on-going dialogue with peers or 'buddies';

- conducting paired observation/planning or inviting feedback on new activities;
- engaging students, TAs and others in observation of aspects of the teaching and learning;
- keeping a journal or a blog;
- engaging with theory through professional and academic materials;
- completing a portfolio of professional learning (or e-portfolio using Mahara, for example);
- enrolling on a Masters programme.

Task 15.3

Vehicles for reflection

Take up to three of the above ideas and investigate the viability of undertaking one or more. For example, if learning on-line has particular appeal, sign up to a blog or set up your own and engage with it for a week or two to see whether it appeals to you as a way of sharing your approaches, ideas and concerns.

One obvious way of reflecting is to engage in teacher research either within your school or as part of, for example, a Masters programme.

HOW CAN RESEARCH HELP YOU?

Classroom research has had to fight for respectability but is now widely accepted at all levels. Many new entrants to the profession will have had the opportunity to engage in aspects of classroom-based research in some form and many will have completed modules at Masters level. Hopefully, research has been demystified and you will recognise the benefits of gathering evidence on which to evaluate the quality of the learning and thereby take ownership. Informally, we are always researching: finding out things, checking information and ideas. What we seldom do is do this systematically. What we need is what Pollard *et al.* (2008) refer to as an 'evidence-informed classroom'.

For classroom research undertaken by practitioners to succeed, it arguably has to satisfy three conditions. It has to address an aspect of learning that:

- you want to change;
- you need to change;
- you can change.

Why the three conditions? Well, first of all, you have to have a desire to change something to see it through. Secondly, there must be a genuine need to change or else, again, you will not carry it out. Thirdly, it must be something that is feasible, that you can realistically change. You may want and need to change Year 11's attitude to French, but how realistic is it for you to do that as a piece of research?

ACTION RESEARCH

The specific research approach described below is ideally suited to the teacher who wants to, needs to and is able to change their practice. It is called action research and it embodies all the features of a good practitioner study, and it is predicated on the desire of the researcher to improve practice through reflection. It is not possible to do justice to action research as a concept here, and apologies to those who might find the description rather instrumental, but the fundamentals of the approach embody many of the strong features of reflective practice and action research.

Fundamentally, it must involve action (some change to practice, incorporation of new materials) and it must use research to inform practice. N.B. Just doing the research is not the 'action' part. Essentially, action research involves following the following steps (although not necessarily in a strict order):

- identify an area;
- define specific goals;
- develop a plan of work;
- develop your recording techniques (data gathering tools);
- evaluate success;
- explain any lack of success and look for remedies;
- aim to repeat the success;
- if possible, disseminate your findings.

The cycle is often presented as a series of cycles or spirals. Central to the planning is the need to identify your goal. As the saying goes, if you do not know where you are going, any road will do and, I would add, you will not know when you get there. It is important to measure the impact of the change and evaluate it systematically rather than resort to 'gut reaction' as to whether the change has worked or not. Paradoxically, the tighter and smaller the focus, the deeper the analysis and the greater the reflection.

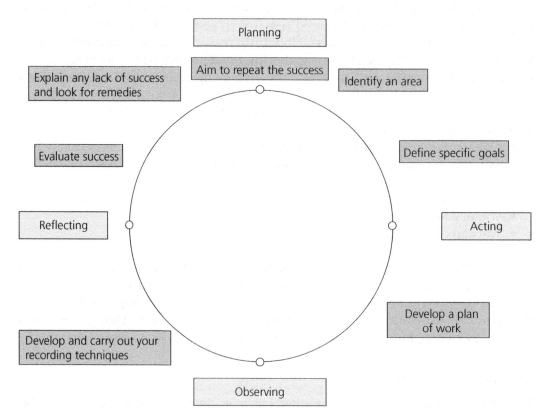

Figure 15.1 The action research cycle

Task 15.4

A case study

Read the case study below and answer the following questions:
Why was the intervention successful?
Could the same outcome have been achieved without the systematic reflection and application of research?

Case study

A teacher of French in a secondary school was concerned about the impact that a teaching assistant (TA) was having on her lessons. The teacher, who was using the target language, was often interrupted by the TA reprimanding the pupils in broad Yorkshire. The focus of the intervention was to reduce the TA's use of English and encourage the use of French in the classroom. The approach adopted was to involve the TA in language presentation at the beginning of each unit of work. The TA was given pronunciation practice and shown how to present the language.

The lessons were audio-recorded before and during the intervention to measure the impact and both the teacher and the TA made diary entries.

The relatively simple intervention proved to be successful on a number of counts. The TA felt more involved and grew in confidence as she was perceived differently by the pupils. A professional dialogue was started on the subject of target language and the TA's role and the interruptions ceased. The teacher went on to ask herself what else the TA could contribute in the target language and to the learning process generally.

The key to any research study is the research question. What do you want to know? Sadly, many teachers as researchers begin with the 'tools', the research methods (questionnaire, interview), often influenced by their practicality or attractiveness rather than their utility, and make the question fit the tools. That is like going to the tool shed, picking the nicest tools or those nearer to hand and *then* deciding what to make. Ask yourself: what do I want to know and how might I economically gather valid and reliable evidence which answers my questions?

It helps if the research is collaborative and that means the learners too. Recognising the value of the social nature of learning, try your best to involve your colleagues and your students. Research *with* them, rather than *on* them for best results and more positive outcomes. The return in terms of informing your practice and sustaining a professional dialogue is potentially great. Look for quick wins and clear benefits since these will motivate and sustain you.

The analysis of evidence and evaluation can often be the weakest elements. Action researchers are all too liable to run out of time or steam, or both, or be satisfied with their achievements without adequate reflection.

Whatever you do, make sure that your classroom-based research is rigorous. It will be, by definition, small-scale and you will not make any claims to generalisability. That is not the point of action research. The point is that you will understand your classroom better and be in a position to improve the learning. You will probably find that you end up with more questions than answers. As Hopkins (2008) says, it is not about knowing all the answers, it is about asking better quality questions.

Task 15.5

Action research cycle

Fill in a potential action research cycle using the prompts.

Identify an area	Which area of your teaching do you need to, want to and are able to change?
Define specific goals	What might be a very small, specific focus for you to work on?
Develop a plan of work	How long is it going to take? Which class(es)/ groups? Whose help are you going to enlist? What research and reconnaissance do you need to carry out first?
Develop your recording techniques	How are you going to record and measure the change (observation, interview)?
Evaluate success	What have been the expected and unexpected outcomes?
Explain any lack of success and look for remedies	What has not quite worked to plan? Why is this? What could you do to put it right?
Aim to repeat the success	If it works well with x, will it work with y? Can I extend the idea to other aspects? Can I share this with colleagues?

Task 15.6

Next steps

Identify sources to consult and actions that you can realistically take now.

For ideas and information

Bookmark and regularly visit key websites, for example:
http://www.all-languages.org.uk/
Get hold of accessible books through organisations.
Join the Association for Language Learning (ALL) as an active member and attend conferences and training events.
Get in touch with your language organisation: Goethe-Institut, Instituto Cervantes, etc.

For action

Work out a sustainable pattern of reflection that suits you and stick to it.
Try to involve colleagues or friends in the same or other institution to work with you.
Involve the pupils – they can surprise you with their insights!
Find out about opportunities for further study.
Find out what support/resources are available within reach.

SUMMARY

The benefits of reflecting, becoming 'research literate' (Heilbronn, 2004) and using evidence-informed practice supported by research are clear. We need teachers who are 'extended professionals' who challenge assumptions and show judgement and social awareness. Reflection is most effective when it is systematic and research provides a structure and vehicle for that reflection.

REFERENCES

Heilbronn, R. (2004) 'Using research and evidence', in Capel, S., Heilbronn, R., Leask, M. and Turner, T. (eds) *Starting to Teach in the Secondary School*. 2nd edition. London: Routledge.

Hopkins, D. (2008) *A Teacher's Guide to Classroom Research*. 4th edition. Maidenhead: Open University Press.

Pollard, A. *et al.* (2008) *Reflective Teaching*. London: Continuum.

Race, P. (2005) *Making Learning Happen*. London: Sage.

Rolfe, G., Freshwater, D. and Jasper, M. (2001) *Critical Reflection in Nursing and the Helping Professionals: A User's Guide*. Basingstoke: Palgrave Macmillan.

USEFUL WEBSITES AND RESOURCES

http://www.tlrp.org Teaching and Learning Research Programme (TLRP) led by Andrew Pollard, a leading expert on teacher reflection.

http://www.rtweb.info An associated website providing supplementary material.

http://www.education.gov.uk/schools/toolsandinitiatives/tripsresearchdigests   TRIPS research digests.

Index